Practical Guide to SAP® Internal Orders (CO-OM)

Marjorie Wright

Thank you for purchasing this book from Espresso Tutorials!

Like a cup of espresso coffee, Espresso Tutorials SAP books are concise and effective. We know that your time is valuable and we deliver information in a succinct and straightforward manner. It only takes our readers a short amount of time to consume SAP concepts. Our books are well recognized in the industry for leveraging tutorial-style instruction and videos to show you step by step how to successfully work with SAP.

Check out our YouTube channel to watch our videos at
https://www.youtube.com/user/EspressoTutorials.

If you are interested in SAP Finance and Controlling, join us at
http://www.fico-forum.com/forum2/
to get your SAP questions answered and contribute to discussions.

Related titles from Espresso Tutorials:

- ▶ Martin Munzel: New SAP® Controlling Planning Interface
  http://5011.espresso-tutorials.com
- ▶ Michael Esser: Investment Project Controlling with SAP®
  http://5008.espresso-tutorials.com
- ▶ Stefan Eifler: Quick Guide to SAP® CO-PA (Profitability Analysis)
  http://5018.espresso-tutorials.com
- ▶ Paul Ovigele: Reconciling SAP® CO-PA to the General Ledger
  http://5040.espresso-tutorials.com
- ▶ Tanya Duncan: Practical Guide to SAP® CO-PC (Product Cost Controlling)
  http://5064.espresso-tutorials.com
- ▶ Ashish Sampat: First Steps in SAP® Controlling (CO)
  http://5069.espresso-tutorials.com
- ▶ Rosana Fonseca: Practical Guide to SAP® Material Ledger (ML)
  http://5116.espresso-tutorials.com
- ▶ Ashish Sampat: Expert Tips to Unleas the Full Potential of SAP® Controlling
  http://5140.espresso-tutorials.com
- ▶ John Pringle: Practical Guide to SAP® Profit Center Accounting
  http://5144.espresso-tutorials.com

Marjorie Wright
Practical Guide to SAP® Internal Orders (CO-OM)

ISBN:	9-781-5371-5970-6
Editor:	Carol Zarrow
Cover Design:	Philip Esch, Martin Munzel
Cover Photo:	istockphoto # 45976702 © Bluefont
Interior Design:	Johann-Christian Hanke

All rights reserved.

1st Edition 2016, Gleichen

© 2016 by Espresso Tutorials GmbH

URL: *www.espresso-tutorials.com*

Feedback
We greatly appreciate any kind of feedback you have concerning this book. Please mail us at *info@espresso-tutorials.com*.

Table of Contents

Preface

Throughout my career, I've found internal orders to be a very flexible cost object. I've also found them to be a bit misunderstood by business users, and often deployed with only the basic configuration.

In this book, I am offering knowledge to both the business user and the technical user on features and benefits of using the internal order. By combining the functional and technical knowledge in one publication, everyone benefits.

Marjorie Wright

We have added a few icons to highlight important information. These include:

Tips

 Tips highlight information concerning more details about the subject being described and/or additional background information.

Examples

 Examples help illustrate a topic better by relating it to real world scenarios.

Attention

 Attention notices draw attention to information that you should be aware of when you go through the examples from this book on your own.

Finally, a note concerning the copyright: all screenshots printed in this book are the copyright of SAP SE. All rights are reserved by SAP SE. Copyright pertains to all SAP images in this publication. For simplification, we will not mention this specifically underneath every screenshot.

1 Introduction

1.1 What is an Internal Order?

Internal orders are cost objects in Controlling-Overhead Management. These cost objects are intended to be used as "temporary cost collectors" for short-term projects or events in the organization. They are not as structured or permanent as cost centers. There is no standard hierarchy for internal orders; however, they can be grouped to meet individual requirements. All the control parameters of these cost objects are determined by the order type—which is configurable.

Compared to cost centers, internal orders are far more flexible and can be utilized to meet many business requirements.

Internal orders have an advantage over cost centers in that we can plan, budget, and use availability control. This allows us to monitor spending for these projects or events by comparing spending to plan, as well as limiting spending against a budget. Think of this as plan equals funds approved and budget equals funds appropriated. These are often different values.

Internal orders again differ from cost centers in their ability to collect cost and revenue and to utilize results analysis to determine profitability.

As business transactions are posted to internal orders, we can analyze that activity in real time by using reports in the information system. From a single report, we can branch to additional reports and accounting documents, as well as view the source document.

At the end of a period, amounts can be allocated from orders to other cost objects by the settlement process. Settlement may be quite simple (to one receiver), or more complex (using extended settlement to allocate to multiple receivers using several tracing factors). Periodic reposting can also be used to allocate cost from internal orders using, for example, statistical key figures.

Internal orders can also be used as statistical cost objects. In this case, there is no further allocation or settlement. We will look at these in more detail in the Special Topics chapter.

1.2 Business Scenarios

SAP supports four distinct business scenarios for internal orders:

- ▶ Overhead orders—these are used to monitor spending until their settlement to one or more cost objects.
- ▶ Investment orders—these are used to monitor spending until their settlement to an asset or assets.
- ▶ Accrual orders—these are used to offset accruals made only in Controlling (an uncommon use).
- ▶ Orders with revenue—these are used when Sales and Distribution is not implemented, and/or to monitor cost and revenue for noncore business activity.

This text will explore overhead orders.

1.3 Why would an organization use an Internal Order?

These are a few examples of when the use of internal orders may be required:

- ▶ If you are managing cost for a company event, the final cost of which will be divided among cost centers.
- ▶ If you want to track spending for a major repair, the final cost of which will be settled to a product line.
- ▶ If you are responsible for a fleet of service vehicles, the final cost of which should reside on a single cost center.
- ▶ If you are managing a capital project with a finite budget.
- ▶ If you need to measure revenue and cost for a nonstandard event.

Each of the above examples would require:

- ▶ An order with control parameters set for actual/plan cost, and a settlement rule or a periodic reposting cycle to cost centers.
- ▶ An order with control parameters set for actual/plan cost, and a settlement rule to a profitability segment.
- ▶ An order with control parameters for statistical cost, and a real cost-center assignment.

▶ An order with an investment profile, a budget, and availability control.

▶ An order with control parameters for revenue, and perhaps a sales order line item assignment.

As you can see, the combinations and possibilities are quite flexible.

1.4 How will this book help me understand Internal Orders?

Our understanding of an order's master data is the foundation. By reviewing the order type configuration, we learn how the business requirement determines the structure of the order master data.

In each of the following chapters, we will first review the business processes of the internal orders used in Controlling-Overhead Management (CO-OM). In this context, a *business process* is what users can see and do on the SAP Easy Access Menu, and the ways these various transactions support the daily needs of the business entity. Next we will review the technical settings required to fulfill the business process. In other words, we will work in the SAP configuration menu. Lastly, each chapter will follow a business example from start to finish.

The chapters are structured according to usual business practices:

Chapter 2 Master Data: In this chapter we will review the creation of the order master data and its importance in the business process, and we will review the configuration steps for the order type and for status management.

Chapter 3 Planning and Budgeting: We will review the process of business planning and budgeting with availability control, and the configuration of these various profiles.

Chapter 4 Daily Postings: We will review the various business transactions for internal orders without revenue, and we will review the configuration steps required.

Chapter 5 Period End Close: We will review the extended settlement of orders and ways to utilize statistical key figures in a periodic reposting. The configuration steps for the settlement profile, allocation and source structure will be reviewed.

Chapter 6 Reporting: We will examine the information system reporting menu and review the creation and use of summarization hierarchies.

Chapter 7 Special Topics: We will review the use of Statistical Orders, Orders with Revenue, and S4/HANA.

1.5   Business Process Example

As we review the business process to be executed on the SAP Easy Access application menu, and as we determine the customizing settings in the Implementation Guide, this will be our example:

Your organization is deploying employee training in new business processes. The training sessions will be held on campus. External training staff will be hired to deliver the sessions. Lunch, break snacks, and beverages will be provided to the attendees. An associate from Human Resources will be responsible for the event execution. Employees from multiple cost centers will attend the training.

These are the organizational requirements:

- ▶ Ability to track all spending on one object
- ▶ Ability to share the total cost among the cost centers, providing as many details as possible
- ▶ Ability to reclassify internal cost to the event
- ▶ Ability to enter purchase orders for the event
- ▶ Manage the event against a plan value
- ▶ Control spending

These are the technical requirements:

- ▶ Internal order type
- ▶ Planning profile
- ▶ Budget profile with availability control
- ▶ HR associate named as the budget manager
- ▶ Extended settlement with multiple rules
- ▶ Activated commitments for internal orders

► Statistical indicator deselected or hidden

► Settlement profile allowing settlement to cost centers

► Settlement allocation structure for transparency

We summarize these requirements in Table 1.1.

Organizational requirements	Technical requirements	Refer to ...
Ability to track all spending on one object	Create an internal order type, disallow statistical order(s)	Chapter 2—Master Data
Ability to share the total cost of the event among cost centers	Extended settlement with multiple distribution rules	Chapter 5—Period End Close
Provide as much transparency as possible to cost centers	Settlement profile with allocation structure	Chapter 5—Period End Close
Ability to track any purchase orders for the event	Commitments active	Chapter 4—Daily Postings
Ability to reclassify internal cost to the event		Chapter 4—Daily Postings
Manage the event to a plan value	Create/assign planning profile	Chapter 3—Planning and Budgeting
Control spending, any overage to attention of HR associate	Create/assign budget profile with AVC and budget manager	Chapter 3—Planning and Budgeting

Table 1.1: Overview of a business process example

2 Master Data

Accurate master data is critical in SAP, and it must exist before any type of posting can occur. In this chapter, we will review the methods of creating master data for internal orders and order type customizing.

2.1 Master data

The object internal order is the master data. The internal order is created from an order type, which contains all the parameters of the object. It is important to select the appropriate order type when you are creating an internal order.

2.1.1 Create an internal order

There are two methods of creating an internal order, and both are found on the SAP Easy Access menu.

To create internal orders from the Order Manager:

ACCOUNTING • CONTROLLING • INTERNAL ORDERS • MASTER DATA • ORDER MANAGER KO04

On the Order Manager screen, select the CREATE ❶ icon (see Figure 2.1).

Use the CREATE INTERNAL ORDER dialog ❷ (enter or use the dropdown to select an order type, then select the ENTER icon).

The CREATE INTERNAL ORDER: MASTER DATA screen will be displayed on the right. On the left, the "find by or search" feature and the Personal Worklist will be displayed. To hide these sections, select the SHOW/HIDE WORKLIST icon ▣ Worklist .

Figure 2.1: Use Order Manager KO04 to create an internal order

To create an internal order **without** Order Manager KO04:

ACCOUNTING • CONTROLLING • INTERNAL ORDERS • MASTER DATA • SPECIAL FUNCTIONS • ORDER • CREATE KO01

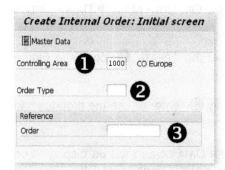

Figure 2.2: Create an internal order from KO01

On the Create Internal Order: Initial screen, enter or use the dropdown to select the controlling area ❶ (see Figure 2.2).

On the Create Internal Order: Initial screen, enter or use the dropdown to select the order type ❷.

Select the MASTER DATA icon 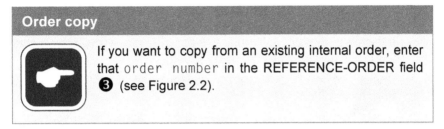Master Data or the ENTER icon (you can also press Enter on your keyboard).

The Create Internal Order: Master Data screen will be displayed.

Order copy

If you want to copy from an existing internal order, enter that order number in the REFERENCE-ORDER field ❸ (see Figure 2.2).

In Figure 2.3, we use order type 0400. This is an SAP standard delivered example of an order type. The order type determines everything about the order: whether there are default values ❸, the order number ❶, the screen layout ❷, any required fields, and so forth. Each organization can create order types with specific settings in support of its business requirements.

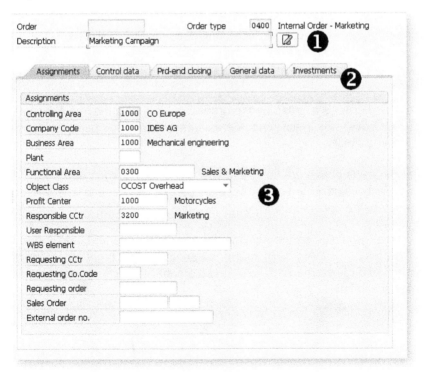

Figure 2.3: Initial data entry screen using order type 0400

We will explore each setting found in this example of an order.

Order header

▶ Order number: This can be entered manually or determined by a number range assigned to the order type. If the field is greyed out, the next number in the range will be determined and assigned to the internal order when it's being saved.

▶ Order type: This field is greyed out and cannot be changed from here.

▶ Description: This value is user defined, according to your business requirements.

Assignments tab

▶ Controlling area: This field is greyed out, and it cannot be changed here. It was determined by the Controlling Area you set in transaction OKKS.

▶ Company code: If it's allowed by the order type, this field may be changed. However, the company code entered must be assigned to the Controlling Area displayed above.

▶ Business area: If it's allowed by the order type, this field may be changed.

▶ Plant: If it's allowed by the order type, this field may be changed. However, the plant must be assigned to the company code entered above.

All of the fields above are important when you're posting to and from the order. Each value entered will become part of the posting and will be recorded at the document level.

The remaining fields on the Assignment tab are for informational purposes. You may use them in reporting, creating groups, creating selection variants, and to automatically assign settlement rules. These features will be discussed later.

Control Data tab

In the STATUS group we find:

▶ System status: The current status is displayed. You may see arrow up and arrow down buttons to manually change the status. These are the standard SAP status indicators for internal orders:

  ▸ REL released—With this status, all business transactions can be performed.

  ▸ TECO technically complete—With this status, limited business transactions can be performed.

  ▸ CLSD close—With this status, just a few activities can occur. CLSD prevents any posting to or from the order.

To see the list of possible business transactions for the current status of an order, select the ALLOWED TRANSACTIONS icon. Additionally, from the System menu select GOTO • STATUS and select the BUSINESS PROCESSES tab. Here you can see the full description of possible business transactions and can sort the list.

If the order type contains a status profile, you may also see a user status in addition to the system status. This could provide more control than the three statuses listed here.

In the CONTROL DATA GROUP we find:

▶ CURRENCY: The system proposes the Company Code currency. If allowed by the order type, this field may be changed.

▶ STATISTICAL ORDER: If selected, the order will be a statistical cost object. In the Special Topics chapter (Chapter 7), we will review the requirements.

▶ PLAN INTEGRATED ORDER: If selected, the order will be integrated with Cost Center and Profit Center Planning. In Planning and Budgeting (Chapter 3), we will deep-dive on these features.

▶ REVENUE POSTINGS: If selected, the order can receive postings on revenue cost elements. In the Special Topics chapter (Chapter 7), we will review the requirements.

- ► COMMITMENT UPDATE: If selected, the order can display purchase commitments. See the Daily Postings chapter (Chapter 4) for details.

- ► ACTUAL POSTED COST CENTER: Use only if the statistical indicator is selected, to specify the true cost center for posting.

Period End Close tab

These settings will be discussed in Period End Close (Chapter 5).

General Data tab

In General Data we find

- ► Applicant, Telephone, Department, etc.

These fields are for information purposes only. You may use them in collective maintenance or as selection variants. The field descriptions may be modified as part of system configuration.

Investments tab

These fields support SAP's Investment Management business processes, and are outside the scope of this text.

Now that we have an understanding of internal orders' master record fields and their use, let's return to our Business Process Example. An order type has been created in the SAP Customizing menu to meet our requirements.

Notice in Figure 2.4 the appearance of the master record compared to its appearance in the example in Figure 2.3.

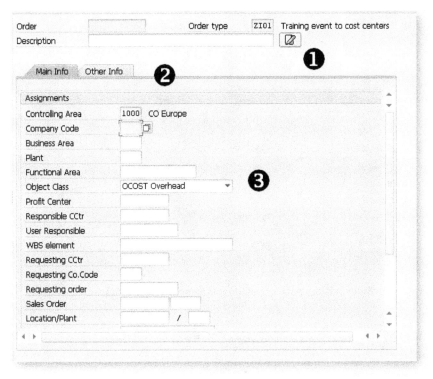

Figure 2.4: Initial data entry screen for order type ZIO1

In Figure 2.4 we see no default description ❶ and fewer tabs ❷. There is also less data entered by default ❸.

Each order type we can select at the time of master data creation can have quite different parameters, as evidenced by this simple example.

For our example, in Figure 2.5 you can see I have entered a description and the relevant values for company code, business area, and profit center on the MAIN INFO tab.

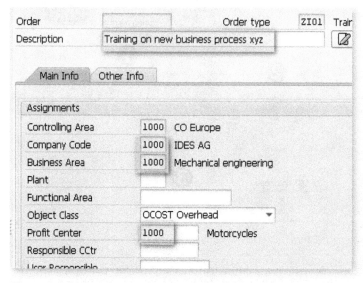

Figure 2.5: Main Info tab of our business process example order

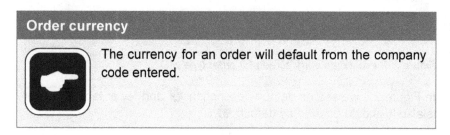

In Figure 2.6 the order status has been set to "released" by using the up/down indicators ❶.

To see all allowed business transactions for the current order status, select the Allowed Transactions pushbutton ❷ shown in Figure 2.6.

Display order status

An alternative method of displaying order status: From the system menu, select Go To, Status. Navigate to the Business Process tab to see the green or red light for each type of transaction.

Figure 2.6: Order status indicators

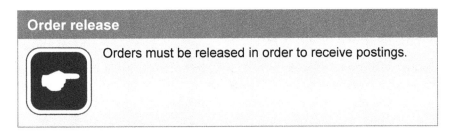

Order release

Orders must be released in order to receive postings.

From Figure 2.7, also note that on the OTHER INFO tab in the CONTROL DATA group, this order has commitments active and there is no selection for Statistical.

Main Info   Other Info

Control data

Currency   EUR   Euro (EMU currency as of

Order category   1   Internal Order (Controlling

Actual posted C

☐ Plan-integrated order

☐ Revenue postings

☑ Commitment update

Figure 2.7: Control data

For now, these basic settings are enough to proceed with using the internal order. Later, we will add the settlement rule we need for Period End Close.

Upon saving the order, the next available number in the number range is assigned. This number displayed in Figure 2.8 becomes the master record identifier for our order. Going forward, postings will be made to this master record number.

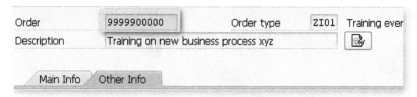

| Order | 9999900000 | | Order type | ZI01 | Training ever |
| Description | Training on new business process xyz | | | | |

| Main Info | Other Info |

Figure 2.8: Order number assigned at saving

2.1.2 Maintain an internal order

Just as with order creation, there are two transactions in the menu that maintain orders individually. These are helpful when the changes are "one offs." Later, we will review mass (collective) maintenance.

If you are using Order Manager KO04, select the order to be maintained and use the CHANGE ∅ pushbutton to make changes, or the DISPLAY ⬥ pushbutton to display an order.

As seen in Figure 2.9, the Order Manager also provides a "copy as" feature ❶ and a "Find by" search section ❷, as well as your worklist ❸ of recently accessed orders.

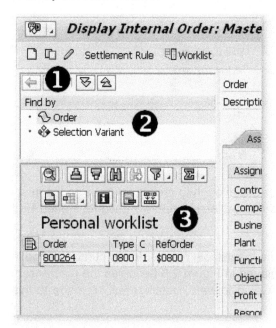

Figure 2.9: Order Manager features

If you are not using Order Manager KO04, you can use the following transactions in the menu:

ACCOUNTING • CONTROLLING • INTERNAL ORDERS • MASTER DATA • SPECIAL FUNCTIONS • ORDER • CHANGE KO02

ACCOUNTING • CONTROLLING • INTERNAL ORDERS • MASTER DATA • SPECIAL FUNCTIONS • ORDER • DISPLAY KO03

2.1.3 Order Groups

Since internal orders do not utilize a standard hierarchy, and since the "number" of the master record is simply the next number in the assigned number range, it can be challenging to group like orders together.

Creating order groups is an especially helpful aid in the planning, reporting, allocation, and collective maintenance of orders.

To manually create an order group:

ACCOUNTING • CONTROLLING • INTERNAL ORDERS • MASTER DATA • ORDER GROUP • CREATE KOH1

In the CREATE ORDER GROUP: INITIAL screen, enter a key for the group.

Group key

This can be up to ten alphanumeric characters with a suffix of up to four more, separated by a period, e.g., 1234567891.abc1

Select the Hierarchy pushbutton, or press ⌞Enter⌟.

In the CREATE ORDER GROUP: STRUCTURE screen, enter a description.

Use the various icons to insert order numbers in the group or to build a hierarchical group structure.

Press ⌞Enter⌟ to validate the order numbers you have entered. The descriptions of the orders will then be displayed as seen in Figure 2.10. Save your group when it's complete.

Figure 2.10: Create order group

A caution on entering order numbers

Entering order numbers horizontally indicates a range of orders.

Validation of order numbers

There is no validation that orders exist in the system. If you enter an order number that either has not been created or is in error, its description will read "no valid master." However, you will be able to save the group.

2.2 Implementation Guide (IMG) Menu Basics

Before we discuss the specific steps to create an order type, let's review some basic features of the Implementation Guide (IMG) menu.

To access this menu from the SAP Easy Access menu:

TOOLS • CUSTOMIZING • IMG • EXECUTE PROJECT SPRO

In the CUSTOMIZING: EXECUTE project screen, select the pushbutton DISPLAY SAP REFERENCE IMG.

The IMG menu contains all the required and optional settings for internal order configuration. Generally, the folders are structured in the order in which you should approach each task.

To display a mandatory activity, from the System menu, navigate to ADDITIONAL INFORMATION • ACTIVITY IMPORTANCE.

To display the transaction code, from the System menu, navigate to ADDITIONAL INFORMATION • ADDITIONAL INFORMATION • DISPLAY KEY • IMG ACTIVITY, as shown in Figure 2.11.

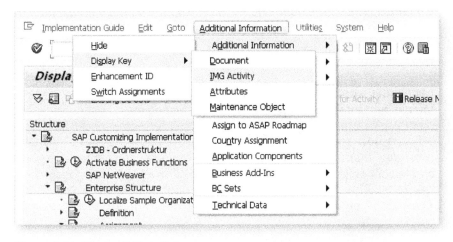

Figure 2.11: Display IMG Activity

Generally, the last four characters of the string represent the transaction code, as shown in Figure 2.12. ❶

Figure 2.12: Transaction code as the last four characters

2.3   Order Type Customizing

SAP provides several standard delivered order types. Examples of common ones are shown in Table 2.1.

Order Type	Description
0300	Internal Order-Tools and Equipment
0400	Internal Order-Marketing
0800	Internal Order-Repair/Maint.
1000	Internal Order-Statistical

Table 2.1: Examples of order types

Each order type is an example of how you might customize your system. Various assignments and profiles will differ among them.

When a new order type is required, you may copy from one of these examples, making changes as needed, or you may begin from scratch to create your settings.

The order type must be assigned to a number range before it can be used for order creation.

Client-level setting

 Note this is an SAP client-level setting. All Controlling Areas of the client may use the same order types.

2.3.1   Create an order type

To create an order type, from the SAP IMG menu:

CONTROLLING • INTERNAL ORDERS • ORDER MASTER DATA • DEFINE ORDER TYPES • KOT2

A list of existing order types is displayed in CHANGE VIEW "ORDER TYPES": OVERVIEW.

To review an existing order type, select the grey box to the left of the order type, and either `double-click` or select the DETAILS icon.

To copy an existing order type, select the grey box to the left of the order type, and select the COPY AS icon.

In the CHANGE VIEW "ORDER TYPES": OVERVIEW, select the CREATE icon to create a new order type.

The order type key and category are assigned when the order type is created.

Internal Orders are created as category 01; select the `category` as shown in Figure 2.13.

Change View "Order Types": Overview

Order categ...	Short Descript.
01	Internal Order (Controlling)
02	Accrual Calculation Order (Cor
03	Model Order (Controlling)
04	CO Production Order

Figure 2.13: Order Category

The order type key is a four-character alphanumeric entry, and the description should clarify how the order type will be used, as shown in Figure 2.14.

New Entries: Details of Added Entries

Order Type	ziol Training event to cost centers
Order category	1 Internal Order (Controlling)
Number range interval	Not assigned

Figure 2.14: Order Type Key and Description

The number range can be assigned either here or in a separate transaction found in the menu.

On the NEW ENTRIES: DETAILS OF ADDED ENTRIES screen, as shown in Figure 2.15, you can assign the parameters of the new order type.

Figure 2.15: New Entries: Details of Added Entries

It is important to have an understanding of each setting in the order type. In the following sections, we will define the purpose of each group noted in Figure 2.15.

Required field

The object class is the only field required when an order type is created. You may assign other settings at any time, as well as assign profiles that already exist in your SAP system. (A profile is a form of a variant, and can be assigned to multiple order types.)

Number range

The order type cannot be used to create internal orders until a number range is assigned.

Changes to existing order types

Order type settings are dynamic, in that a change affects existing master records in the SAP system.

General parameters group ❶

▶ PROFILES: the various profiles will be discussed in later sections of this text.

▶ OBJECT CLASS: Set this as "overhead costs."

▶ FUNCTIONAL AREA: A default functional area can be assigned. All orders created from this order type will default to this value when the order is created.

▶ MODEL ORDER: Other default values can be assigned using a model order. Navigate to the subfolder SCREEN LAYOUT • DEFINE MODEL ORDERS KO02.

Model Order Category

Note that model orders use category $$ and are created within a controlling area.

Control indicators group ❷

▶ CO Partner update. This setting affects how the totals record tables used in the information system are updated by a "partner" during overhead allocations.

   ▶ Active: Totals records are updated for each partner combination.

   ▶ Semi-active: Totals records are updated for order combinations only.

   ▶ Not active: No totals records are produced.

▶ Classification. Allows orders to be selected in the information system.

▶ Commit. Management. Allows purchase requisition and purchase order values to be displayed in the order information system.

▶ Revenue postings. Allow orders to accumulate revenue.

▶ Integrated planning. Allows integration with Cost Center and Profit Center Planning (see more details in the planning section).

Archiving group ❸

▶ Residence time 1: Calendar months between setting the delete flag and the final deletion indicator.

▶ Residence time 2: Calendar months between setting the final deletion indicator and reorganizing.

Master data display group ❹

▶ Order layout: Assign an order layout here to determine the screen layout of the order. Navigate to the subfolder SCREEN LAYOUT • DEFINE ORDER LAYOUTS to create tab titles and to position data groups on each tab.

► Field selection: Select the EDIT icon to maintain the field status of the order master record.

Page down to see all available fields. Fields that have been hidden appear in blue text. You can also make these settings by order type in the subfolder SCREEN LAYOUT • SELECT FIELDS.

Status management group ❺

When you're reviewing or copying from existing, older order types, you may see two radio buttons for status management: GENERAL STATUS MANAGEMENT and ORDER STATUS MANAGEMENT (now obsolete). When you're creating new order types, you will see neither radio button.

These are the standard SAP status indicators for internal orders:

REL released: With this status, all business transactions can be performed.

TECO technically complete: With this status, limited business transactions can be performed.

CLSD closed: With this status, just a few activities can occur. CLSD prevents any posting to or from the order.

► STATUS PROFILE. Here you can assign more detailed user status indicators. You can create the profile in the subfolder Status Management-Define Status Profiles.

► RELEASE IMMEDIATELY. Orders will have the status REL upon creation, allowing all business transactions to access them.

► STATUS DEPENDENT FIELD SELECT. Used in combination with a status profile to set the order master data field status based on the status number in the profile.

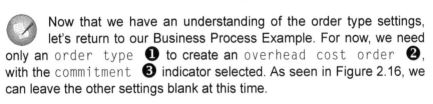 Now that we have an understanding of the order type settings, let's return to our Business Process Example. For now, we need only an order type ❶ to create an overhead cost order ❷, with the commitment ❸ indicator selected. As seen in Figure 2.16, we can leave the other settings blank at this time.

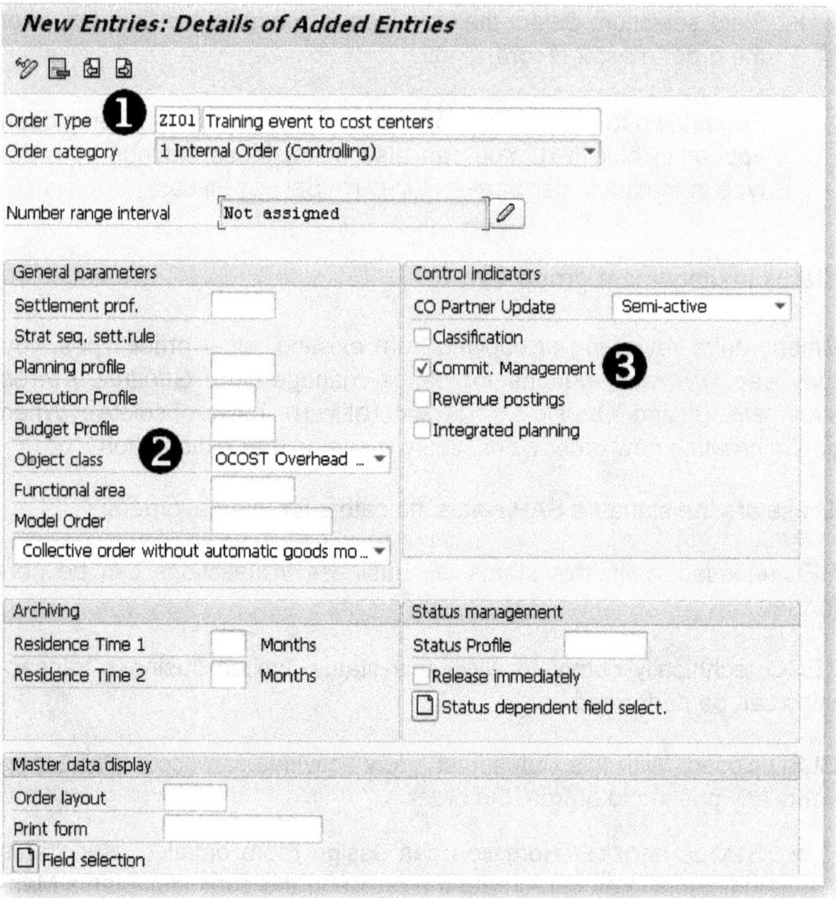

Figure 2.16: Order type to meet our Business Process Example

Number range message

Upon saving the order type, you will receive a message regarding the missing number range. Continue through the message, as we will add this in a later step.

Number range

The order type cannot be used to create internal orders until a number range is assigned.

2.3.2   Create an order number range

Each internal order must be uniquely identified by an *order number*. The order number must be assigned to the internal order master record, either manually by the user at creation or automatically upon saving for the first time.

When number ranges are created, you determine the range, as well as indicating if the numbers are externally assigned.

To create a new number range, from the SAP IMG menu:

CONTROLLING • INTERNAL ORDERS • MAINTAIN NUMBER RANGES FOR ORDERS • KONK

On the RANGE MAINTENANCE: ORDER screen, select the DEFINE GROUPS pushbutton.

On the GROUP MAINTENANCE: NUMBER RANGE AUFTRAG screen, select the CREATE pushbutton.

Enter a range of numbers broad enough to support your requirements.

The SAP system will assign the next available group number to your range in the leftmost field (in Figure 2.17, it is 36).

To assign numbers manually at the time of order creation, you may enter an alphanumeric range and select the `External Assignment` checkbox. When users manually enter the order number, it must be within this range.

Maintain Intervals: Order

| Group | Number Range for new orders |

| Object | AUFTRAG |
| Subobject | |

Ranges

No	From No.	To Number	NR Status	Ext
36	009999900000	009999999999	0	

Figure 2.17: Create group for number range

Once the number range has been created, it must be assigned to the order type.

To assign a new number range, from the SAP IMG menu:

CONTROLLING • INTERNAL ORDERS • MAINTAIN NUMBER RANGES FOR ORDERS • KONK

On the RANGE MAINTENANCE: ORDER screen, select the DEFINE GROUPS pushbutton.

On the GROUP MAINTENANCE: NUMBER RANGE AUFTRAG screen, select the CREATE pushbutton.

The display will first list all order types that are not assigned a number range. These will be described as NON-ASSIGNED ELEMENTS. Below the non-assigned order types, the display will list all number ranges by group and show all order types assigned to each group.

❶ From the NON-ASSIGNED ELEMENTS, select your order type by clicking it once.

❷ Next, select the ASSIGN ELEMENT/GROUP pushbutton as seen in Figure 2.18.

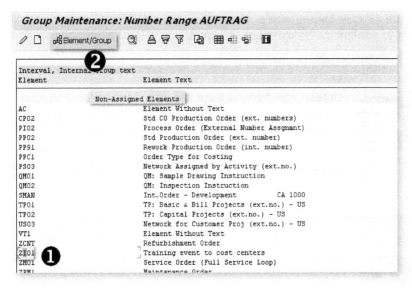

Figure 2.18: Assign an order type to an element or group

From the group selection list, select your number range as seen in Figure 2.19, and continue.

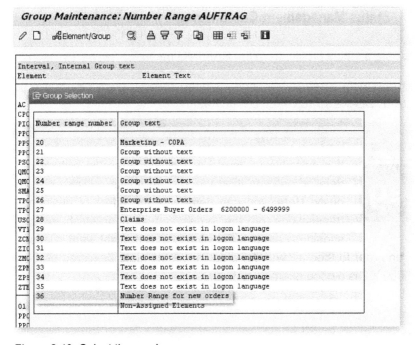

Figure 2.19: Select the number range

On the GROUP MAINTENANCE: NUMBER RANGE AUFTRAG screen, scroll down to confirm the assignment and save.

How many number ranges are needed?

Unless you have a business requirement for a unique numbering scheme, a number range can be assigned to multiple internal order types. Ensure the range is broad enough to support the volume of orders expected to be created over time.

Client level settings

Number ranges are SAP client level settings.

2.4 Status Management Customizing

To create a status profile, from the SAP IMG menu:

CONTROLLING • INTERNAL ORDERS • ORDER MASTER DATA • STATUS MANAGEMENT DEFINE STATUS PROFILES • OK02

User status is an optional setting

It is possible to create a user status profile with more detailed settings than the system status outlined previously. Here, you can determine the effect of business transactions on the order status, and which action should occur next. For example, you might want release of an order to then allow order planning. A standard delivered profile 00000002 is a good example of this.

2.5   Screen Layout Customizing

In this section, we can change the structure and appearance of the order master record.

2.5.1   Field Status

To determine the field status of the order type, from the SAP IMG menu:

CONTROLLING • INTERNAL ORDERS • ORDER MASTER DATA • SCREEN LAYOUT • SELECT FIELDS

Position ▣ Position... to your order type, select the row, and either double click or select the DETAILS pushbutton.

In the Order Master Data display group, select the CHANGE FIELD SELECTION icon as seen in Figure 2.20.

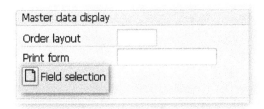

Figure 2.20: Master Data Display: Field Selection

From here, you can page through the available fields to determine whether the field is to be hidden, is for display only, is ready for input, or is required.

Page down for additional fields

! In the bottom left corner, there is a page indicator. Be sure you continue to page down through the list of modifiable fields.

Display technical names

 To display the technical names of the fields, from the System Menu select UTILITIES • TECHNICAL NAMES.

User status dependency

 Field status may also depend on the order status. If a user status profile has been assigned to an order, make these settings in the Status Management group of that order.

Change Field Selection

Order Type   ZI01 Training event to cost centers

Modifiable fields

	Hide	Display	Input	Req. entry	HiLi
Department	○	○	⊙	○	☐
Description	○	○	⊙	○	☐
End of Work	○	○	⊙	○	☐
Entered by	○	○	⊙	○	☐
Estimated total costs of order	○	○	⊙	○	☐
External order number	○	○	⊙	○	☐
Functional Area	○	○	⊙	○	☐
G/L account for basic settlement	○	○	⊙	○	☐
Group of disallowed transactions	○	○	⊙	○	☐
Identifier "Revenue posting allowed"	○	○	⊙	○	☐
Identifier for planning with line items	○	○	⊙	○	☐
Identifier for statistical order	⊙	○	○	○	☐
Identifier for work permit issued	○	○	⊙	○	☐
Indicator for Integrated Planning	○	○	⊙	○	☐
Interest Profile	○	○	⊙	○	☐
Investment measure profile	○	○	⊙	○	☐

Page   2 of   5

Figure 2.21: Change field selection

From our Business Process Example, we will not create statistical internal orders using our order type. In the field selection view, page down to find the row Identifier for Statistical Order. Select the HIDE radio button for this row, as shown in Figure 2.21.

2.5.2 Screen Layout

In this setting, we can change the position of groups of fields, and remove unnecessary tabs from the order master record.

We are configuring a new order type that will never be used for assets or investment measures. Also, extended settlement is a requirement, so the period end tab will not be needed. We want those tabs hidden so users are not confused.

To create a screen layout for an order type, from the SAP IMG menu:

CONTROLLING • INTERNAL ORDERS • ORDER MASTER DATA • SCREEN LAYOUT • DEFINE ORDER LAYOUTS

In the CHANGE VIEW LAYOUTS: OVERVIEW screen, select the NEW ENTRIES pushbutton.

Enter a key and description for the layout and press Enter.

Select the layout by clicking the grey box to the left of the key.

From the DIALOG STRUCTURE screen on the left, navigate to the folder TAB PAGE TITLES, as shown in Figure 2.22.

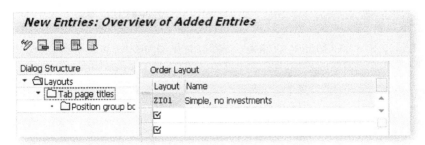

Figure 2.22: Select Tab page titles folder

Here, again select the NEW ENTRIES pushbutton.

Now you can begin to design your layout. There are five tab choices and twelve field groups to position among the tabs. We want to keep our example simple, with two tabs and field groups.

Use the DROPDOWN to assign a tab page number (1-5), and enter its title as seen in Figure 2.23.

Press [Enter].

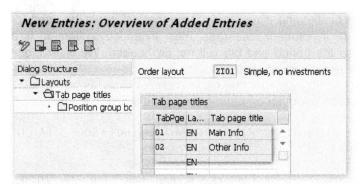

Figure 2.23: Assign tab pages and titles

Next, as seen in Figure 2.24, select a tab page row, and navigate in the DIALOG STRUCTURE on the left to the POSITION GROUP BOXES folder.

Select NEW ENTRIES pushbutton.

From the DROPDOWN, select a position (1–5) ❶

From the DROPDOWN, select a group box (1–12) of fields ❷

Continue in this manner until all required field groups are assigned to each tab.

Save.

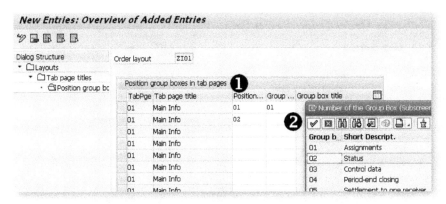

Figure 2.24: Choose position and group box

To assign the Order Layout, enter the layout in the order type setting under Master Data Display, as shown in Figure 2.25.

CONTROLLING • INTERNAL ORDERS • ORDER MASTER DATA • DEFINE ORDER TYPES • KOT2

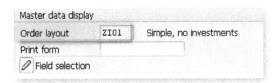

Figure 2.25: Assign the layout to an order type

2.5.3 Model Orders

Model orders allow you to assign various default settings to all orders created with an order type containing the model order key. Common uses are to assign default Business Area, Profit Center, and Functional Area, as seen in Figure 2.26.

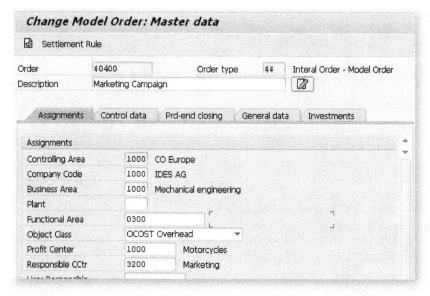

Figure 2.26: Model order $0400

Additional functions

Models orders are created within a Controlling Area and may have default settlement parameters. They are a special order type category: $$.

To create a model order, from the SAP IMG menu:

CONTROLLING • INTERNAL ORDERS • ORDER MASTER DATA • SCREEN LAYOUT • DEFINE MODEL ORDERS

To assign a model order to an order type, from the SAP IMG menu:

CONTROLLING • INTERNAL ORDERS • ORDER MASTER DATA • DEFINE ORDER TYPES • KOT2

Enter the model order in the GENERAL PARAMETERS group.

Model Order conflicts

There may be a conflict between the settings on an order type and a model order. For example: The functional area on a model order will overwrite the functional area on an order type. Also, screen layouts are not affected by model orders—however, carefully test any impact that field status may have when it's used with a model order.

2.6 Selection and Collective Processing Customizing

In this section, we find selection variants and rules for collective processing.

2.6.1 Selection Variants

Since internal orders do not utilize a standard hierarchy, and since the "number" of the master record is simply the next number in the assigned number range, it can be challenging to group like orders together.

Using selection variants can simplify the task of grouping like orders for the purposes of collective processing and collective displaying.

Transactions that can use selection variants

On the SAP application menu:

▶ Collective processing manually KOK2

▶ Collective processing automatically KOK4

▶ Collective display KOK3

To create a selection variant, from the SAP IMG menu:

CONTROLLING • INTERNAL ORDERS • ORDER MASTER DATA • SELECTION AND COLLECTIVE PROCESSING • DEFINE SELECTION VARIANTS OKOV

In the `variant` field, enter a maximum of fourteen alphanumeric characters to identify the variant, and select the CREATE icon.

As shown in Figure 2.27, on the EDIT VARIANTS: VARIANT XYZ screen, you will see all internal order master data fields and several key figures. Enter the appropriate values in all the field(s) to ensure internal orders will be selected.

Edit Variants: Variant 123456789ABCDE

Attributes

Order group					
Order		to			
Order type		to			
External order number		to			
Short text		to			
Assignments					
Controlling area					
Company code		to			
Business area		to			
Plant		to			
Functional area		to			
Object Class		to			
Profit center		to			
Responsible cost center		to			
User Responsible		to			
Requesting company code		to			
Requesting cost center		to			
Requesting order		to			
WBS Element		to			
Sales order		to			

Figure 2.27: Some of the fields available for variant use

To select based on legal entity

eg In the ASSIGNMENTS group, enter a single company code, a range of company codes, or a list using multiple selections.

When your selection criteria are complete, select the ATTRIBUTES Attributes pushbutton in the upper left of the screen.

On the variant attributes screen, you can enter a description of the variant and assign other parameters, such as background processing and protection, as shown in Figure 2.28.

Variant Attributes

✏ Use Screen Assignment ℹ

Variant Name	123456789ABCDE
Description	my variant

☐ Only for Background Processing
☐ Protect Variant
☐ Only Display in Catalog
☐ System Variant (Automatic Transport)

🖨 🖩 🔍 🖨 🔩 Technical name

Objects for selection screen

	Selection Screen	Field name	Type	Protect field	Hi
	1,000	Order group	P	☐	
	1,000	Order	S	☐	
	1,000	Operation/Activity	S	☐	
	1,000	Order type	S	☐	
	1,000	External order number	C	☐	

Figure 2.28: Variant Attributes

Save your entries and exit.

2.6.2 Collective Processing

From the application menu, users can maintain internal orders collective-ly using Collective Processing-Automatically KOK4. There, an option is given as a FUNCTION SELECTION to apply a substitution rule to execute the required changes.

How can a substitution rule be used?

Let's assume we are utilizing the person responsible and business area fields on our internal order master re-cords. For business area 1000, Mr. Jones should be the person responsible and for business area 4000, Ms. Smith should be the person responsible. However, as time has passed, our master data input has not been consistent and other values have been entered. By creating a substitution rule to re-place the values for person responsible based on the business area, we can automate the maintenance task and standardize the data.

Substitution rules are SAP Client-level objects. They can have multiple steps; each with a prerequisite (e.g., business area=1000) and a substitution (e.g., person responsible=Jones).

The rule is called from within the KOK4 transaction when processing and will be applied only to the internal orders also selected there by a selection variant.

To read more on substitution, from the SAP IMG menu:

CONTROLLING • INTERNAL ORDERS • ORDER MASTER DATA • SELECTION AND COLLECTIVE PROCESSING • MAINTAIN SUBSTITUTION RULES FOR COLLECTIVE PROCESSING OKOU

3 Planning and Budgeting

Planning and budgeting are distinct functions in SAP. The features can be used together or can stand alone. Internal orders may have Plan and Budget values. In this chapter, we review both of these optional features

3.1 Basic Planning for Internal Orders

Planning allows a comparison of committed funds against planned values. Planning for an internal order allows analysis of actual/plan/variance in the information system. There are several levels of planning:

- ▶ Overall values—here, you can plan at a high level by year or in more detail by unit costing, cost element, and activity input.
- ▶ Planner Profile—here, you can assign layouts for very specific planning data entry for two planning areas: Cost and Activity Inputs, and Statistical Key Figures.

3.1.1 Overall Planning

We will explore the overall values method, as it is used more often than other methods when planning order spending.

To enter plan values using the overall values method, from the SAP Easy Access menu:

ACCOUNTING • CONTROLLING • INTERNAL ORDERS • PLANNING • OVERALL VALUES • CHANGE • KO12

On the CHANGE OVERALL PLANNING: INITIAL SCREEN enter your order number as seen in Figure 3.1 and press Enter.

Plan by group

Note that you can also plan for an order group.

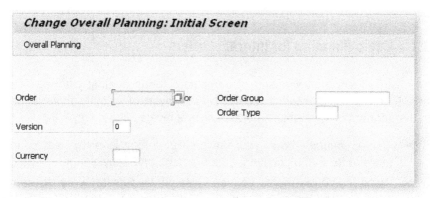

Figure 3.1: Overall planning order entry

On the CHANGE ORDER PLAN VALUES: ANNUAL OVERVIEW screen seen in Figure 3.2, you can enter plan values as overall ❶ and/or by year ❷. There is no validation that the sum of the years equals the total.

Planning on this screen is not very useful, as most reports in the information system are by cost element.

To plan by primary cost element, place your cursor in the ANNUAL VALUES PLAN field for the year you want to plan, and select the Primary Costs pushbutton ❸, as seen below.

Position cursor in the year to be planned

To plan by cost element, you must first position your cursor in the year to be planned, then select the PRIMARY COSTS pushbutton.

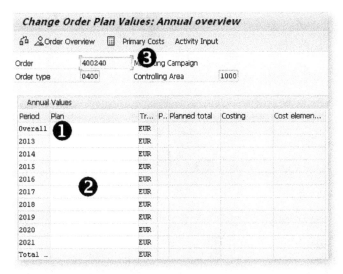

Figure 3.2: Planning annual overview screen

Currency

The currency used for planning is determined in Customizing. In our example, we are planning in euros, which is the Controlling Area currency.

As seen in Figure 3.3, on the CHANGE PLANNING PRIMARY COSTS: OVER-VIEW screen you can enter total plan cost by primary cost element. Scroll down for additional cost elements ❶. The cost elements available for planning are determined by the planning profile assigned to the order type.

The value being planned is for the entire year ❷. Select the appropriate distribution key from the dropdown ❸ as seen in Figure 3.3.

How to use a distribution key

The distribution key controls the way the planned value is spread over the plan periods. Use the dropdown to select the method by key.

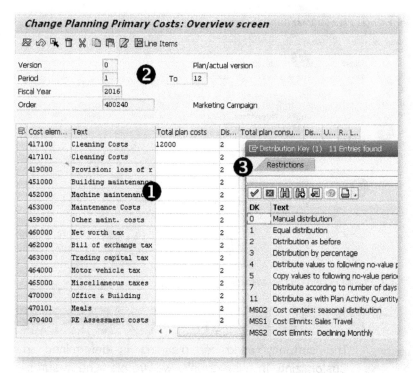

Figure 3.3: Planning by primary cost element

When complete, save the plan data.

On the CHANGE ORDER PLAN VALUES: ANNUAL OVERVIEW screen, save your data again.

From our Business Process Example, we want to plan the spending anticipated for the training event. In Figure 3.4, you can see three expenses planned for 2016 against our order. Note that distribution key 1 was used, which will divide the planned values evenly over the periods planned.

To plan by period

In some cases, planning needs to be executed by period. There may be shortened timelines for the orders, or perhaps the distribution keys are not specific enough. In these cases, place your cursor on the value and select the PERIOD SCREEN pushbutton 🖾 for a display as seen in Figure 3.5. You may overtype any value in the display.

Change Planning Primary Costs: Overview scre

☒ ⌂ ⬚ 🗑 ✂ 📋 📑 🗒 🗓 Line Items

Version	0		Plan/actual version
Period	1	To	12
Fiscal Year	2016		
Order	9999900000		Training on new b

Cost elem...	Text	Total plan costs	Dis...	Tot
476400			2	
476500	Misc. admin. costs		2	
476900	Miscellaneous costs	200.00	1	
477000	Advertising & Sales		2	
477001	Congresses, seminars		2	
477050	Instructor Fees	2,500.00	1	
477055	Training Material	500.00	1	
477100	Advertising items		2	

Figure 3.4: Planned cost for our example of an order

Change Planning Primary Costs: Period screen

⚇ ⌂ ⬚ ✂ 📋 📑 🗒 🗓 Line Items

Version	0	Plan/actual version
Fiscal Year	2016	
Order	9999900000	Training on new business
Cost Element	477050	Instructor Fees

P...	Text	Total plan costs	Total plan consu...	U...	R..	L..
1	January	208.33			☐	☐
2	February	208.34			☐	☐
3	March	208.33			☐	☐
4	April	208.33			☐	☐
5	May	208.34			☐	☐
6	June	208.33			☐	☐
7	July	208.33			☐	☐
8	August	208.34			☐	☐
9	September	208.33			☐	☐
10	October	208.33			☐	☐
11	November	208.34			☐	☐
12	December	208.33			☐	☐
*Pe		2,500.00	0.000			

Figure 3.5: Plan values by period

3.2 Planning Profile Customizing

To create a Planning Profile, from the SAP IMG menu:

CONTROLLING • INTERNAL ORDERS • PLANNING • MANUAL PLANNING • MAINTAIN PLANNING PROFILES FOR OVERALL PLANNING • KAPL

In the SELECT ACTIVITY dialog, select DEFINE PLANNING PROFILE FOR OVER-ALL PLANNING.

On the CHANGE VIEW "COST PLANNING FOR CO ORDERS: PLAN PROFILE": OVERVIEW screen you can select NEW ENTRIES or COPY AS to create your own profile.

In the PROFILE field, enter a six-character alphanumeric key and description for the profile.

Let's use an SAP standard delivered example to explore each field setting. In Figure 3.6 you can see profile 000001 General Budget/Plan Profile as a reference for the following:

Time frame

- ▶ Past: How many years in the past you can plan
- ▶ Future: How many years in the future you can plan
- ▶ Start: The start year will be calculated as the current fiscal year plus this value

---

Start year usage

 The past and future years are calculated based on the start year.

- ▶ Total values: Select to allow planning of overall values
- ▶ Annual values: Select to allow overall planning by year

Representation

▶ Decimal places: Enter the number of decimal places to be displayed as output

Detailed planning and unit costing

Settings below SAP client level

 Note that some selections here are made within a chart of accounts and a controlling area.

▶ Prim.CElem.grp: Enter the chart of accounts and cost element group that can be planned for

▶ Revenue CE grp.: Enter the chart of accounts and the revenue cost element group that can be planned for

▶ Sender CC tr group: Enter the controlling area and the sender cost center group for activity planning

▶ Sender act.type grp: Enter the controlling area and the sender activity type group for activity planning

▶ Stat. key fig. group: Enter the controlling area and the statistical key figure group that can be planned

▶ Costing Variant: Enter a costing variant for use in unit cost planning

Currency Tranl., Overall Plan Values

▶ Exch. Rate Type: Used to translate multicurrency planning

▶ Value Date: Used to determine the exchange rate

Planning Currency

Here you can select the currency in which the plan values are to be entered.

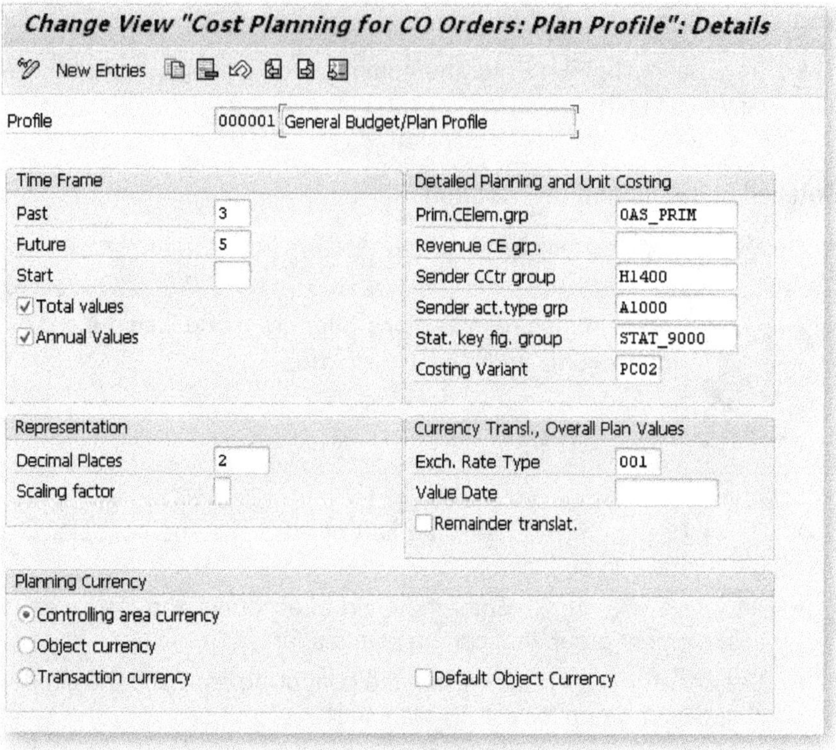

Figure 3.6: SAP delivered planning profile example

When your planning profile has been completed and saved, it must be assigned to the order type.

CONTROLLING • INTERNAL ORDERS • PLANNING • MANUAL PLANNING • MAINTAIN PLANNING PROFILES FOR OVERALL PLANNING • KAPL

From the SELECT ACTIVITIES dialog, choose MAINTAIN PLANNING PROFILE FOR ORDER TYPES.

In the CHANGE VIEW ORDER TYPES: OVERVIEW, a list of internal order types will be displayed. Here you can assign the planning profile to an order type.

From our Business Process Example, we need only a very simple planning approach. The SAP standard delivered planning profile 000001 General Budget/Plan Profile is sufficient. In Figure 3.7, I have selected the dropdown to assign it to our order type ZIO1.

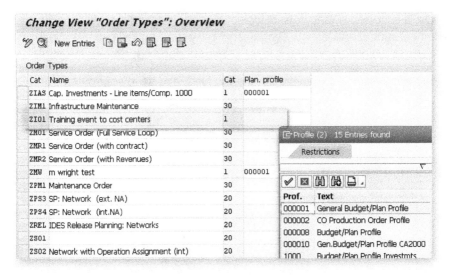

Figure 3.7: Assign plan profile to an order type

3.3 Budgeting for Internal Orders

Budgeting allows a tight control of funds as budgeted value is consumed. Spending can be halted based on the consumption of budget. Budgeting, when combined with availability control (*AVC*) for an internal order, allows for the control of spending. This is quite different from the planning feature we saw in Section 4.2. Planning is a "soft" metric, allowing for the analysis of actual spending compared to plan. Budgeting can limit actual spending.

To enter initial budget values for the order, from the SAP Easy Access menu:

ACCOUNTING • CONTROLLING • INTERNAL ORDERS • BUDGETING • ORIGINAL BUDGET • CHANGE • KO22

On the CHANGE ORIGINAL BUDGET: INITIAL SCREEN, enter your order number and press [Enter].

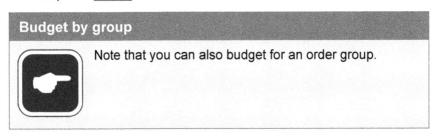

Budget by group

Note that you can also budget for an order group.

On the CHANGE ORIGINAL BUDGET: ANNUAL OVERVIEW SCREEN, you can enter budget values as overall and by year. Unlike in order planning, there is validation that the sum of the years does not exceed the total.

Enter the annual and overall budget values, and save your data.

Annual vs. periodic budgeting

Unlike planning, budgeting is not possible by period.

Add comments

To add texts or notes related to the transaction, select the DOCUMENT TEXT pushbutton. Text can also be added after posting by using the document change KO2A transaction in the menu.

Original, supplement, return

A complete business process can be built around the additional menu options for Supplement and Return.

Overall budget values vs. budget values by year

It is possible to enter only an overall budget amount without entering budget values by year. This could cause AVC to be inaccurate.

From our Business Process Example, we want to budget the spending anticipated for the training. Our planned cost was 3200 euros and was entered by cost element. Our budget will be slightly more, 4000 euros, and will be an annual value.

In Figure 3.8, observe the budgeted value for our event.

Change Original Budget: Annual overview

⬚ ▨ ⚲ Order Overview

Order	9999900000	Training on new business process xyz	
Order type	ZI01	Controlling Area	1000

Annual Values

Period	Budget	Tr...	Current bud...	Planned total...
Over...	4,000.00	EUR	4,000.00	
2014		EUR		
2015		EUR		
2016	4,000.00	EUR	4,000.00	3,200.00
2017		EUR		
2018		EUR		
2019		EUR		
Tota...	4,000.00	EUR	4,000.00	3,200.00

Figure 3.8: Budgeted value

Plan value vs. budgeted value

There is no SAP system requirement for these to be equal. In fact, in our regular business process these values are often quite different. Consider planning as "funds requested" and budgeting as "funds approved."

When should budgeting be used?

Most often, budgets are used with capital spending, or larger, long-term projects where funds are finite. Smaller events, such as our text example, typically are not budgeted.

3.4 Budgeting and Availability Control Customizing

To use these features, you first need a Budget Profile. The design of the Budget Profile is similar to the design of the Planning Profile in Section 3.2. Next, you will need to create the tolerance limits for each Budget Profile. Lastly, a Budget Manager must be assigned to the Order Type. If any of these steps are missed or set up incorrectly, availability control will be unusable.

3.4.1 Budget Profile

To create a Budget Profile, from the SAP IMG menu:

CONTROLLING • INTERNAL ORDERS • BUDGETING AND AVAILABILITY CONTROL • MAINTAIN BUDGET PROFILE • OKOB

In the SELECT ACTIVITY dialog, select MAINTAIN BUDGET PROFILE.

On the CHANGE VIEW "BUDGET PROFILE FOR CO ORDERS": OVERVIEW screen, select NEW ENTRIES.

In the PROFILE field, enter a six-character alphanumeric key and description for the profile.

Let's use an SAP standard delivered example to explore each field setting. In Figure 3.9 you can see the profile 000001 General Budget Profile as a reference for the following:

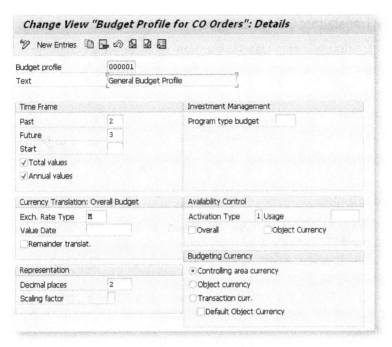

Figure 3.9: Budget profile 000001 General Budget Profile

Time Frame

▶ Past: How many years in the past you can plan

▶ Future: How many years in the future you can plan

▶ Start: The start year will be calculated as the current fiscal year plus this value

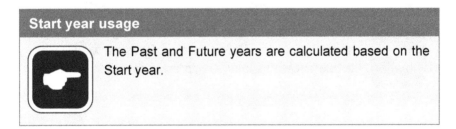

Start year usage

The Past and Future years are calculated based on the Start year.

▶ Total values: Select to allow budgeting of overall values

▶ Annual values: Select to allow budgeting by year

Currency Translation: Overall Budget

- ▶ Exch. Rate Type: Used to translate multicurrency budgeting
- ▶ Value date: Used to determine the exchange rate

Representation

- ▶ Decimal places: Enter the number of decimal places to be displayed as output

Availability Control

- ▶ Activation Type: There are three choices available in the dropdown. To activate availability control automatically when a budget value is saved, select option 1 Automatic activation during budget allocation.
- ▶ Overall: Select this indicator if you want availability control executed against the overall budget value, rather than the annual budget value(s).
- ▶ Object currency: Select this indicator if you want availability control executed in the object currency.

Budgeting Currency

Here you can select in which currency the budget values are to be entered.

Messages when saving

When saving, you may receive a warning message that no tolerances have been entered. Because we will create tolerances in a later step, press Continue.

3.4.2   Maintain Order Type

CONTROLLING • INTERNAL ORDERS • BUDGETING AND AVAILABILITY CONTROL • MAINTAIN BUDGET PROFILE • OKOB

From the SELECT ACTIVITIES dialog, choose MAINTAIN BUDGET PROFILE IN ORDER TYPES.

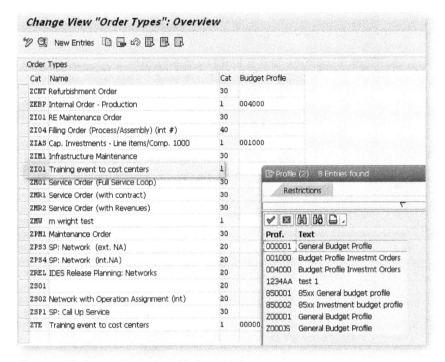

Change View "Order Types": Overview

New Entries

Order Types			
Cat	Name	Cat	Budget Profile
ZCNT	Refurbishment Order	30	
ZEBP	Internal Order - Production	1	004000
ZI01	RE Maintenance Order	30	
ZI04	Filling Order (Process/Assembly) (int #)	40	
ZIAS	Cap. Investments - Line items/Comp. 1000	1	001000
ZIM1	Infrastructure Maintenance	30	
ZI01	Training event to cost centers	1	
ZM01	Service Order (Full Service Loop)	30	
ZMR1	Service Order (with contract)	30	
ZMR2	Service Order (with Revenues)	30	
ZMW	m wright test	1	
2PM1	Maintenance Order	30	
ZPS3	SP: Network (ext. NA)	20	
ZPS4	SP: Network (int.NA)	20	
ZREL	IDES Release Planning: Networks	20	
ZS01		20	
ZS02	Network with Operation Assignment (int)	20	
ZSP1	SP: Call Up Service	30	
ZTE	Training event to cost centers	1	00000

Profile (2)   8 Entries found

Restrictions

Prof.	Text
000001	General Budget Profile
001000	Budget Profile Investmt Orders
004000	Budget Profile Investmt Orders
1234AA	test 1
850001	85xx General budget profile
850002	85xx Investment budget profile
Z00001	General Budget Profile
Z000JS	General Budget Profile

Figure 3.10: Assign budget profile to order type

In the CHANGE VIEW ORDER TYPES: OVERVIEW, a list of internal order types will be displayed. Here you can assign the budget profile to an order type, then save your work.

In our Business Process Example, we need only a very simple budgeting approach. The SAP standard delivered budget profile 000001 General Budget Profile is sufficient. In Figure 3.10, I have selected the dropdown to assign it to our order type ZIO1.

3.4.3   Define Tolerance Limits for Availability Control

The tolerance limits are the most important setting in adequately controlling spending.

To create tolerance limits for a budget profile, from the SAP IMG menu:

CONTROLLING • INTERNAL ORDERS • BUDGETING AND AVAILABILITY CONTROL • DEFINE TOLERANCE LIMITS FOR AVAILABILITY CONTROL • OKOC

In the CHANGE VIEW "ORDER AVAILABILITY CONTROL: TOLERANCE LIMITS": OVERVIEW SCREEN, select the NEW ENTRIES pushbutton.

Enter the Controlling Area and Budget Profile for which you want to create tolerances.

Settings below client level

Order types are created at the SAP client level, but these limits for availability control are set within a controlling area for each budget profile. You may find you need additional budget profiles to maintain different limits within a single controlling area.

Change View "Order Availability Control: Tolerance Limits": Overview

New Entries

Order Availability Control: Tolerance Limits

COAr	Prof.	Tr.Grp	Act.	Usage in %	Abs.variance	Crcy	
1000	000001	++	1	95.00		EUR	
1000	000001	++	2	105.00		EUR	
1000	000001	++	3	115.00		EUR	
1000	001000	++	1	95.00		EUR	
1000	001000	++	2	105.00		EUR	
1000	004000	++	1	95.00		EUR	
1000	004000	++	3	100.00		EUR	

Figure 3.11: Tolerance limits

Use Figure 3.11 with controlling area 1000, profile 000001 as a guide for the structure of these fields:

Tr.Grp: You can restrict the availability control feature by activity. For example, if this rule should be applied only to goods issues, select 03 Goods Issues from the dropdown.

A tolerance group is required

This is a required field. To allow all activities, select ++.

Act.: There are three possible availability control actions: 1, a warning to the user; 2, a warning to the user and e-mail to the budget manager; 3, an error message (this will be a hard stop for the posting).

Usage: Here you enter a budget usage rate as a percentage. This will be the trigger for the warning.

Use of warning action 1

 To cause a warning to the user when the funds committed exceed 80% of the budget, enter Action 1 and Usage 80.

Abs. Variance: Maximum permissible absolute variance; if funds committed exceed the budget by this amount, the selected action will occur. The currency will default as the Controlling Area currency.

Use of absolute variance

 If the budget is 5000 euros and the absolute variance is 300 euros, the appropriate action will be triggered when funds committed exceed 5300 euros.

Percentage and absolute

 If both a usage percentage and an absolute variance are entered, the system will apply the more restrictive.

Continue assigning the three actions as needed, then save your work.

Exempt cost from AVC

 It is also possible to exempt cost elements from AVC. Use the transaction Specify Exempt Cost Elements from Availability Control-OPTK to enter these settings.

3.4.4   Maintain Budget Manager

The last important step is to assign a Budget Manager to the Order Type. This is the person who will be notified via workflow or the SAP Business Workplace Inbox when the AVC action 2 is triggered. This is an SAP user ID.

To assign a Budget Manager, from the SAP IMG menu:

CONTROLLING • INTERNAL ORDERS • BUDGETING AND AVAILABILITY CONTROL • MAINTAIN BUDGET MANAGER • OK14

In the CHANGE VIEW "ORDER AVAILABILITY CONTROL: TOLERANCE LIMITS": OVERVIEW SCREEN, select the NEW ENTRIES pushbutton.

As seen in Figure 3.12, enter the Controlling Area, the Order Type and the SAP user ID of the person who will receive the notifications at action 2.

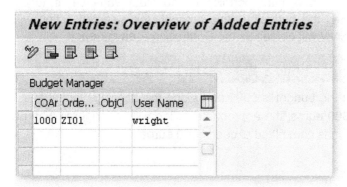

Figure 3.12: Assign SAP user ID as budget manager

Document number ranges

You will need number ranges for planning and budgeting documents: Maintain Number Ranges for Overall Planning OK11

4 Daily Postings

Once the internal order master data has been created, we can begin to accumulate cost on the order. Let's review some of the postings that may occur during the accounting period.

4.1 Posting cost to an Internal Order

The internal order, as a real cost object, collects costs from various sources throughout the accounting period. With each business transaction, the user enters the appropriate internal order number. If the order status allows posting, the posting will be completed and the various accounting documents will be created.

> **Follow your company policy**
>
> Most organizations have strict rules regarding information posted on Financial-Controlling (FI-CO) documents. These examples focus only on a successful posting to our internal order. Always follow your company policy and procedures.

4.1.1 Posting from Financial Accounting

To create a posting to an internal order from a Financial Accounting transaction, simply enter the internal order number in the field ORDER.

 From our Business Process Example: We needed to create a journal entry to record a petty cash expense. We procured items such as coffee and snacks for the training event. The funds were taken from petty cash to pay for these items. Using a financial accounting posting, create a journal entry to expense the items to the internal order and relieve petty cash.

To create the journal, from the SAP Easy Access menu:

ACCOUNTING • FINANCIAL ACCOUNTING • GENERAL LEDGER • DOCUMENT ENTRY • ENTER G/L ACCOUNT DOCUMENT • FB50

Other FI transactions

 You can use any other posting transaction in the Financial Accounting Menu by following this example.

Enter the company code for the posting when you're prompted.

On the basic data tab, enter dates, reference, and texts as per your organization's requirement.

In the item section of the screen, enter the appropriate general ledger (GL) accounts. Remember that cost objects are required if the GL account is linked to a primary cost element in management accounting.

In our example, we want to debit the Misc. Cost GL account with the expense for the internal order, and credit the petty cash GL account as the offset.

Company policies

 Most organizations have strict rules regarding information posted on a financial accounting document. This example focuses only on a successful posting to our internal order. Always follow your organization's policy.

In Figure 4.1 we can see the values entered in FB50, and the internal order number entered in the order field.

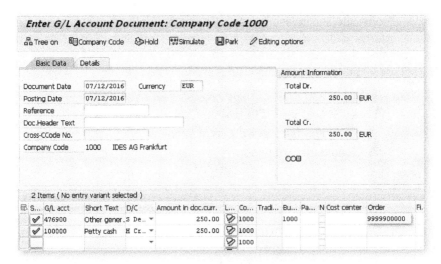

Figure 4.1: Enter the internal order number in FB50

When the document has been posted successfully, a message similar to the one in Figure 4.2 will appear at the bottom of your screen.

☑ Document 100000003 was posted in company code 1000

Figure 4.2: Result of a successful posting

The values are immediately available for analysis in reports of the SAP system. If your reports are outside of the SAP system, the next update will make the values available. We will review reporting examples in Reporting.

4.1.2 Posting from within Controlling

Within management accounting (Controlling) it is possible to re-post cost among real cost objects. This type of transaction will always have a sender cost object and a receiver cost object. The cost element used for the posting may be a primary cost element or a secondary cost element. The transaction used for the re-posting determines which category of cost element may be used.

From our Business Process Example, we need to charge the internal order for the cost of the Human Resources employee who is managing the event. We've determined that the value of his time is 200 euros. Post the transaction on the primary cost element for salaries.

Other methods

An overhead activity allocation or a CATS time sheet could also be used.

To create the reposting, from the SAP Easy Access menu:

ACCOUNTING • CONTROLLING • INTERNAL ORDERS • ACTUAL POSTINGS • MANUAL REPORTING OF COSTS • ENTER • KB11N

On the entry data tab, enter dates and texts as per your organization's requirement.

As displayed in Figure 4.3, use the dropdown menu to select 10-SAP All as the SCREEN VARIANT. ❶

The INPUT TYPE should be S-Individual. ❷

In the document item section, enter cost element 430000 and the amount $200. ❸

Entering comments

 You may also enter a text for reference.

In the OLD ACCOUNT ASSIGNMENT section, enter the sending cost center, in this case Human Resources 2200. ❹

In the NEW ACCOUNT ASSIGNMENT section, enter the receiving internal order number. ❺

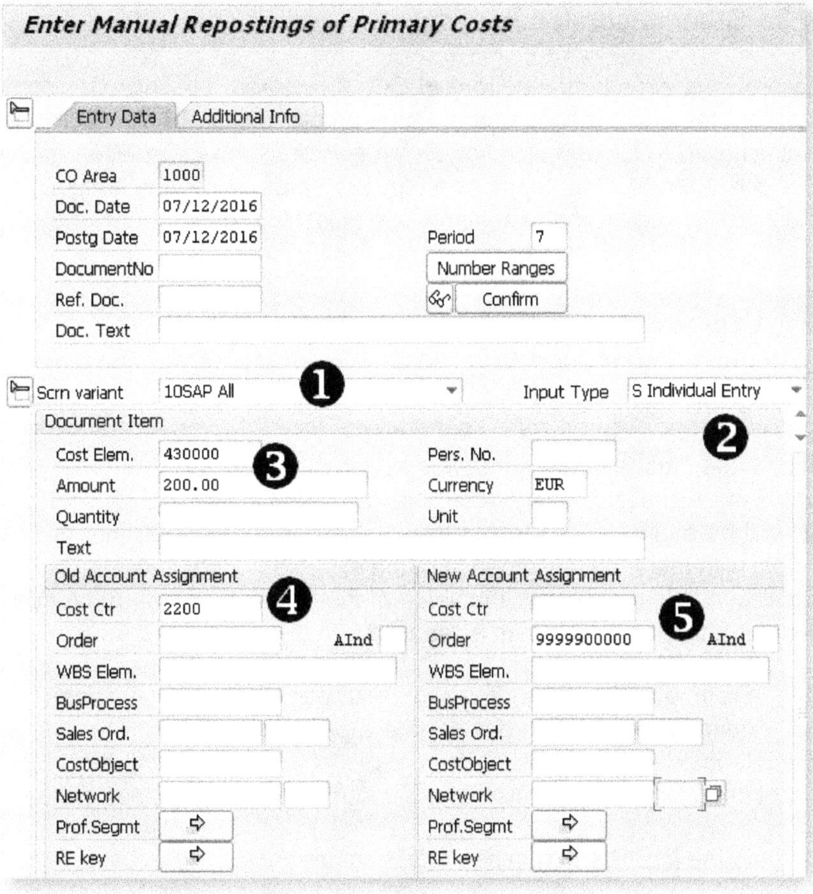

Figure 4.3: Manual reposting

When the document has been posted successfully, a message similar to the one in Figure 4.4 will appear at the bottom of your screen.

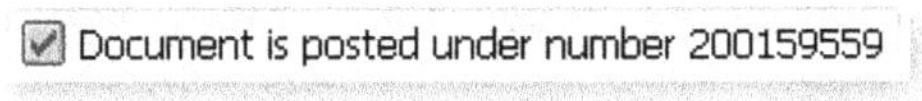

✅ Document is posted under number 200159559

Figure 4.4: Result of successful reposting

The values are immediately available for analysis in reports of the SAP system. If your reports are outside of the SAP system, the next update will make the values available. We will review reporting examples in Reporting.

4.1.3   Other Integrated Postings

The previous examples are from FI-CO. If required, postings can origi-
nate from materials management. For example, using MB1A with move-
ment type 261-Consumption for an order from the warehouse, simply
enter the internal order number when prompted. Also, the transaction
MIGO can be used with the settings Goods Issue and Order.

4.2   Using commitments with an Internal Order

By using the Commitment feature, it is possible to analyze the value of
open purchase orders for an internal order. When the purchase order is
created, the internal order number is assigned at the purchase order item
level. Before the goods are received, the value of the purchase order
item will be available as a commitment in the Internal Order Information
System with the accounting period of the expected goods receipt. Once a
goods receipt has occurred, the value of the GR is assigned to the internal order and the commitment is reduced.

From our Business Process Example, our external printer requires a purchase order. Create a purchase order for the training
materials in the amount of 1500 euros. We expect this delivery in the
current period. Assign the internal order number to the purchase order.

To create the logistics purchase order, from the SAP Easy Access menu:

LOGISTICS • MATERIALS MANAGEMENT • PURCHASING • PURCHASE ORDER •
CREATE • VENDOR/SUPPLYING PLANT KNOWN • ME21N

Enter the Vendor Number and Purchasing Organization information in
the header as per your organizational requirements.

As seen in Figure 4.5, on the first row of the purchase order, enter the
ACCOUNT ASSIGNMENT CATEGORY F-Order.

In the order item section of the screen, navigate to the ACCOUNT ASSIGN-
MENT tab. Enter your internal order number in the Order field as seen in
Figure 4.6.

Figure 4.5: Enter "F" as the account assignment category

GL account assignment

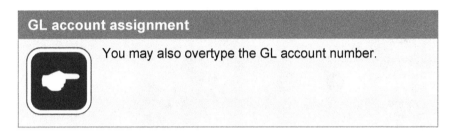

You may also overtype the GL account number.

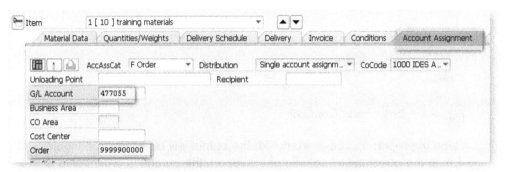

Figure 4.6: Enter the GL account and the internal order number

When the document has been posted successfully, a message similar to the one in Figure 4.7 will appear at the bottom of your screen.

☑ Standard PO created under the number 4500017291

Figure 4.7: Purchase order number assigned upon saving

The values are immediately available for analysis in reports of the SAP system. If your reports are outside of the SAP system, the next update will make the values available. We will review these reporting examples below. You can find additional reporting features in Chapter 6.

To execute a report for internal order commitments, from the SAP Easy Access menu:

ACCOUNTING • CONTROLLING • INTERNAL ORDERS • INFORMATION SYSTEM • REPORTS FOR INTERNAL ORDERS • PLAN/ACTUAL COMPARISONS • ADDITIONAL KEY FIGURES• ORDERS: ACTUAL/PLAN/COMMITMENTS S_ALR_87012999

As seen in Figure 4.8, enter the selection values ❶ for controlling area, periods, and year. In the selection group, enter the single order value ❷.

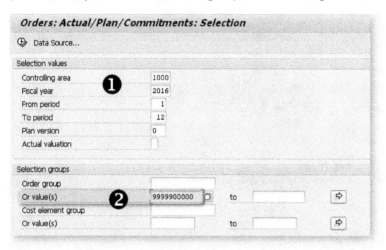

Figure 4.8: Order report selections

Once the report has been executed, the output will be as seen in Figure 4.9. In the COMMITMENT column of the report, the purchase order value is displayed ❶. Notice the report columns for ACTUAL + COMMITMENT = ASSIGNED ❷ and that ASSIGNED is then compared to PLAN to result in AVAILABLE ❸.

Orders: Actual/Plan/Commitments	Date: 07/12/2016 04:30:19			Page: 2 / 4	
Order/Group 9999900000 Training on new business process xyz					
Reporting period 1 - 12 2016					

Cost elements	Actual	Commitment	Assigned	Plan	Available
430000 Salaries - base wages	200.00		200.00		200.00-
476900 Miscellaneous costs	250.00		250.00	200.00	50.00-
477050 Instructor Fees				2,500.00	2,500.00
477055 Training Material		1,500.00	1,500.00	500.00	1,000.00-
* Costs	450.00	1,500.00	1,950.00	3,200.00	1,250.00
** Balance	450.00	1,500.00	1,950.00	3,200.00	1,250.00

Figure 4.9: Actual/Plan/Commitment report output

What about our budget?

This report does not compare actual costs to budget. Later, we will see additional reports and features.

When the logistics goods receipt occurs, the commitment is relieved and the FI-CO posting occurs to valuate the receipt.

The report output is affected immediately by the logistics goods receipt. In Figure 4.10 we can see the COMMITMENT has been relieved and the ACTUAL ❶ values have been updated by the posting.

Orders: Actual/Plan/Commitments		Date: 07/12/2016 04:47:56			Page: 2 / 4
Order/Group	9999900000	Training on new business process xyz			
Reporting period	1 - 12 2016				

Cost elements	Actual	Commitment	Assigned	Plan	Available
430000 Salaries - base wages	200.00		200.00		200.00-
476900 Miscellaneous costs	250.00		250.00	200.00	50.00-
477050 Instructor Fees				2,500.00	2,500.00
477055 Training Material	❶ 1,500.00		1,500.00	500.00	1,000.00-
* Costs	1,950.00		1,950.00	3,200.00	1,250.00
** Balance	1,950.00		1,950.00	3,200.00	1,250.00

Figure 4.10: Actual/Plan/Commitment report output

Be aware

In the information system, the commitment will appear in the accounting period of the expected goods receipt on the purchase order item. If a partial quantity is received and the purchase order item is not fully delivered, the commitment remains active.

4.3 Commitment Customizing

First, each Controlling Area must allow commitments. Then each order type must also have the indicator set.

4.3.1 Controlling Area

Commitments are activated within a Controlling Area.

To activate, from the SAP IMG menu:

CONTROLLING • GENERAL CONTROLLING • ORGANIZATION • MAINTAIN CONTROLLING AREA • OKKP

From the SELECT ACTIVITY dialog, choose `maintain controlling area`

In the OVERVIEW OF CONTROLLING AREAS section, select your controlling area (in our example, 1000)

On the left, in the basic data section, select the `activate components/control indicators` folder as seen in Figure 4.11.

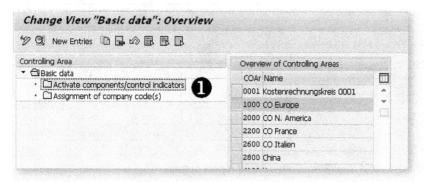

Figure 4.11: Controlling area setting

In the ACTIVATE COMPONENTS section, select `components active` for the COMMIT. MANAGEMENT selection, as seen in Figure 4.12.

Controlling Area	1000	CO Europe	
Fiscal Year	1994	to	9999

Activate Components		
Cost Centers	1 Component active	▼
☐ AA: Activity Type		
Order Management	1 Component active	▼
Commit. Management	1 Components active	▼
ProfitAnalysis	4 Component active for both types of Profitability Analysis	▼
Acty-Based Costing	2 Component Active for Parallel and Integrated Calculation	▼

Figure 4.12: Activate commitment management

4.3.2   Order type

To maintain the order type indicator, from the SAP IMG menu:

CONTROLLING • INTERNAL ORDERS • ORDER MASTER DATA • DEFINE ORDER TYPES • KOT2

Select your order type.

In the CONTROL INDICATORS section, select the checkbox for Commit. Management, as seen in Figure 4.13.

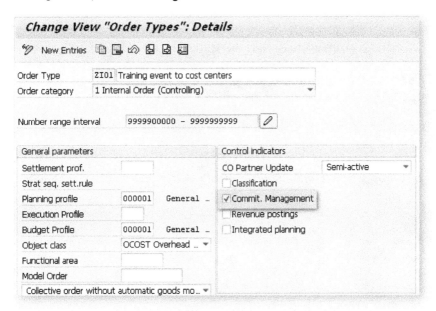

Figure 4.13: Order type commitment indicator

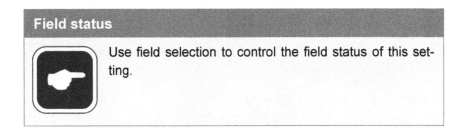

Field status

Use field selection to control the field status of this setting.

4.4 Budget consumption

As we've reviewed the types of daily postings that can be made to an internal order, we have been consuming the budgeted value.

In section 3.3, we created an original budget in the amount of 4000 euros. To date, we have consumed 1,950 euros through various postings to the order.

To confirm our position, from the SAP Easy Access menu:

ACCOUNTING • CONTROLLING • INTERNAL ORDERS • INFORMATION SYSTEM • REPORTS FOR INTERNAL ORDERS • MORE REPORTS • LIST: BUDGET/ACTUAL/COMMITMENTS S_ALR_87013019

Enter a controlling area and valuation view in the SELECTION VALUES ❶ group as seen in Figure 4.14.

Enter your order number in the OR VALUES ❷ field of the selection group, as seen in Figure 4.14.

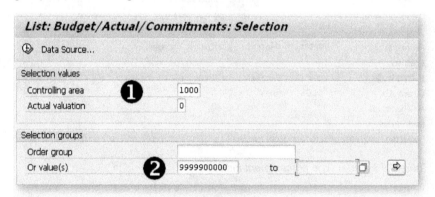

Figure 4.14: Execute Budget/Actual report

In the LIST: BUDGET/ACTUAL/COMMITMENTS view, navigate to the current year ❶, as seen in Figure 4.15.

Notice that the values on the right side of the report now reflect the current year's consumption of budget, as well as budget and commitment values, ❷ as seen in Figure 4.15.

Figure 4.15: Budget/Actual/Commitments report

From our Business Process example, we now have several miscellaneous vendor invoices to post against our internal order. First, let's review our availability control settings for consumption of budget. There are three actions triggered by consumption of budget, as shown in Table 4.1.

	Action	Consumption
1	Warning to user	95%
2	Warning to user, e-mail to budget manager	105%
3	Error	115%

Table 4.1: Availability control tolerance

Table 4.2 displays the value for each action based on the budget value from our previous posting of 4000 euros.

	Action	Consumption
1	Warning to user	3,800€
2	Warning to user, email to budget manager	4,200€
3	Error	4,600€

Table 4.2: Consumption as a value

Our current order balance of 1950 euros is well within the first action consumption of 3800 euros.

However, we now have additional costs to post. Our first will be an invoice for the external training fees in the amount of 2301 euros.

Posting in FB60, our entry would be as seen in Figure 4.16, using the internal order number as the cost object.

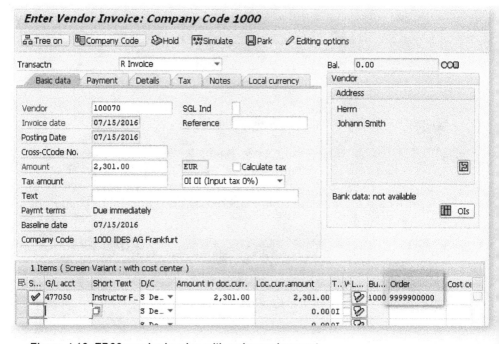

Figure 4.16: FB60 vendor invoice with order assignment

When the document is posted, availability control will check the budget consumption including the value of this document. If one of the three actions is triggered, as seen in Figure 4.17, a message will be displayed on the status bar ❶.

Open the message to read the details ❷, as seen in Figure 4.17. Here we can see that this posting will trigger action 2: Consumption will equal 3851 (1950 + 1901), which is 251 or 106.28%, just over the tolerance of 105%.

> **Posting the document**
>
> Once the warning is triggered, be sure you continue until a document number is displayed on the status bar.

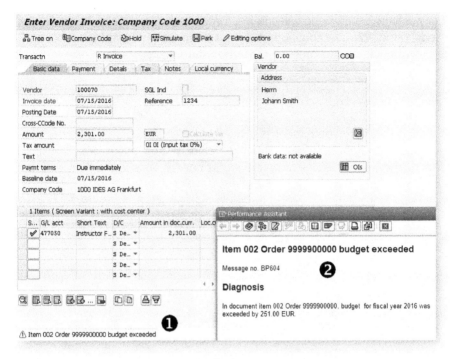

Figure 4.17: Message control warning for budget consumption

The budget manager could receive an email notification from message control. In Figure 4.18 we can see a simulation of the "email" in the SAP Business Workplace inbox. The budget manager can now take appropriate action.

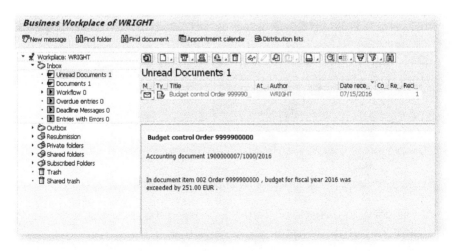

Figure 4.18: Simulation of e-mail to budget manager

If postings continue to the internal order, the tolerances will be applied each time. We can continue until the consumption would trigger action 3. At that point, an error message will be returned.

We have now received another invoice from the trainer for travel expenses in the amount of 350 euros.

Again, when the document is posted, availability control will check the budget consumption, including the value of this document. The error message will be displayed on the status bar ❶, as seen in Figure 4.19.

Open the message to read the details ❷, as seen in Figure 4.19. Here we can see that this posting will trigger action 3: consumption will equal 4601 (4251 + 350) which is 601 or 115.03%, just over the tolerance of 115%.

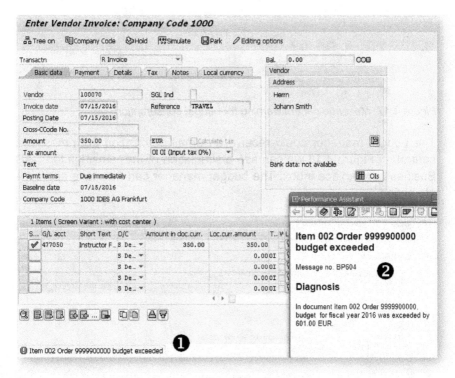

Figure 4.19: Message control error for budget consumption

At this point, the user is blocked from posting the document and should contact the budget manager.

Aside from the report seen earlier in Figure 4.15, there is very little information available on the application menu for users. From the ORIGINAL BUDGET DISPLAY-KO23 transaction, we can get an overview of the settings that control budget and availability control.

From the SAP Easy Access menu:

ACCOUNTING • CONTROLLING • INTERNAL ORDERS • BUDGETING • ORIGINAL BUDGET • DISPLAY KO23

Enter the internal order number and select the original budget pushbutton.

On the DISPLAY ORIGINAL BUDGET: ANNUAL OVERVIEW screen, you can get the big picture of budget, actual, and plan values, as seen in Figure 4.20.

Display Original Budget: Annual overview

🔁 👤 Order Overview

| Order | 9999900000 | Training on new business process xyz |
| Order type | ZI01 | Controlling Area | 1000 |

Annual Values

Period	Budget	Tr...	Current bud...	Assigned	Planned total...
Over...	4,000.00	EUR	4,000.00	0.00	0.00
2014		EUR			
2015		EUR			
2016	4,000.00	EUR	4,000.00	4,251.00	3,200.00
2017		EUR			
2018		EUR			
2019		EUR			
Tota...	4,000.00	EUR	4,000.00	4,251.00	3,200.00

◄ ►

Figure 4.20: KO23 Display budget

From here, navigate to EXTRAS • AVAILABILITY CONTROL • AVAILABILITY CONTROL INFO, as seen in Figure 4.21.

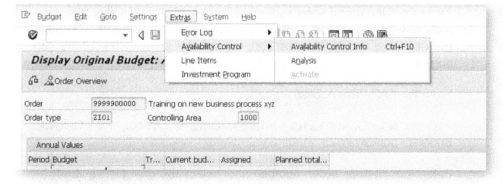

Figure 4.21: Availability control info

The activation settings, as seen in Figure 4.22, will be displayed.

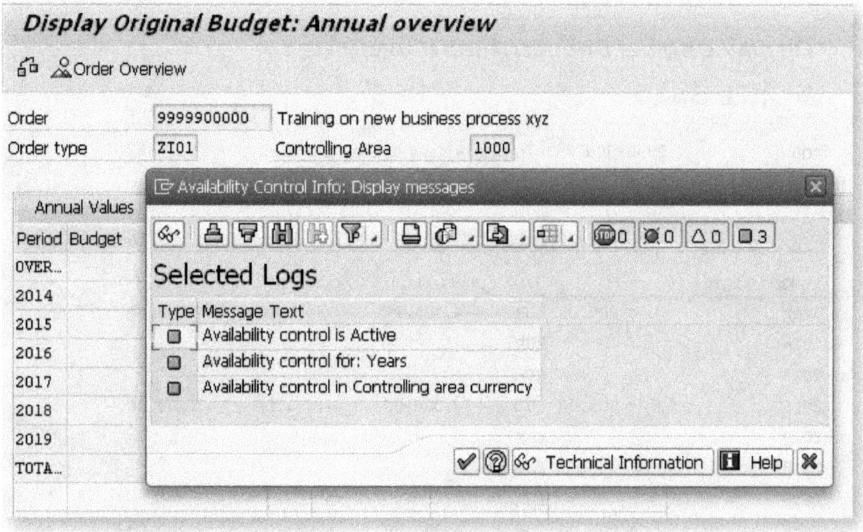

Figure 4.22: Activation settings

Now, navigate to EXTRAS • AVAILABILITY CONTROL • ANALYSIS, and confirm the fiscal year if prompted.

On THE ANALYSIS ACTIVE AVAILABILITY CONTROL screen, more details are available, as seen in Figure 4.23.

Place your cursor on the order type row and in the upper left corner, select the expand subtree icon 📮.

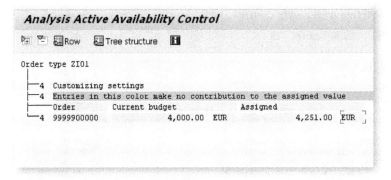

Figure 4.23: Analysis active availability control

Now you can view any exempt cost elements, the action and tolerance assignments (Figure 4.24), as well as an overview of postings (Figure 4.25).

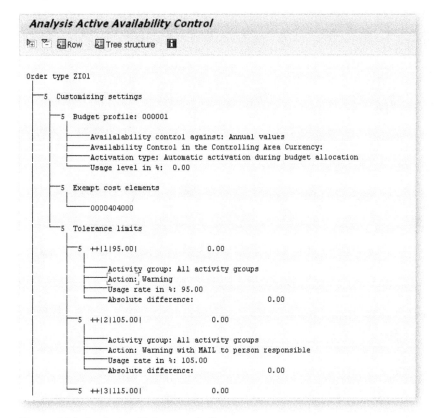

Figure 4.24: Analysis of tolerance limits

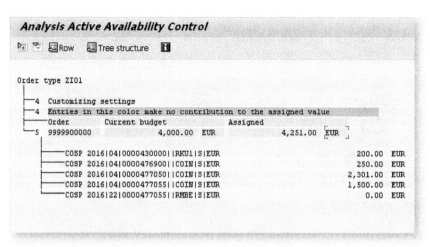

Figure 4.25: Analysis of postings

5 Period End Close

Throughout the accounting period, we have accumulated costs on the internal order. At the period end we want to correctly assign the costs to the responsible cost objects. Any real cost object can be the receiver of these overhead allocations.

In this chapter, let's review several methods available for periodic overhead allocation.

5.1 Periodic Reposting

The periodic reposting method uses SAP's cycle/segment design. It is used when the tracing factor (the value used to spread the cost) is more specific than those available in the settlement process.

In each periodic reposting segment, you must identify the sender and receiver cost objects, the amount of the sender cost to allocate, and the tracing factor for the allocation.

Repost using an SKF

 It is common to collect costs such as electricity on an internal order. At period end, we know how many kilowatt hours our production cost centers consumed. We post these as a statistical key figure (SKF) with reference to the cost center. In the periodic reposting segment, the SKF is assigned as the tracing factor and the production cost centers are assigned as the receivers. When the cycle is executed, the internal order costs are allocated proportionally by kwh to each cost center.

Periodicity

Periodic reposting is executed at period end. The posting can be reversed and re-executed.

To create a periodic reposting cycle, from the SAP Easy Access Menu:

ACCOUNTING • CONTROLLING • INTERNAL ORDERS • PERIOD-END CLOSING • SINGLE FUNCTIONS • PERIODIC REPOSTING KSW5

Select EXTRAS • CYCLE • CREATE to create the cycle and add segments.

To execute a periodic reposting cycle, from the SAP Easy Access Menu:

ACCOUNTING • CONTROLLING • INTERNAL ORDERS • PERIOD-END CLOSING • SINGLE FUNCTIONS • PERIODIC REPOSTING KSW5

Enter the Controlling Area, Period and Year to allocate and the Cycle identification.

Background processing is recommended.

Test Run can be selected.

To reverse a cycle, from the SAP Easy Access menu select PERIODIC REPOSTING • REVERSE.

5.2 Periodic Reposting Customizing

The customizing options for this method allow control of the sender/receiver types. Within each cycle, each segment has a tab "senders/receivers." We can also control whether the fields are allowed and whether single values, ranges, or groups can be used.

This setting is found in the Cost Center Accounting menu.

Changes here affect cost centers and internal orders

 Sender/receiver types and the selection of input values affects both cost objects as they share this setting.

To determine sender/receiver types, from the IMG menu:

CONTROLLING • COST CENTER ACCOUNTING • ACTUAL POSTINGS • PERIOD-END CLOSING • PERIODIC REPOSTING • DETERMINE SENDER/RECEIVER TYPES FOR PERIODIC REPOSTING

A list of fields and an indicator for actual or plan will be displayed. Select DETAILS to see the field attributes as seen in Figure 5.1.

Change View "Customizing Field Attributes: Allocation": Details

Get Standard Values ◀ ▶ 🖨

Allocation type	Periodic reposting
Actual/plan	Actu...
Field	Order

Field attributes

Active status	Entry readiness		Entry readiness		Entry readiness	
Sender	+ SingleVals	X	Interval	X	Group	X
Receiver	+ SingleVals	X	Interval	X	Group	X

Figure 5.1: Field attributes

The possible entries for each attribute are shown in Figure 5.2

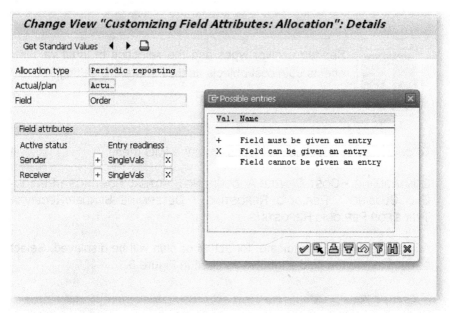

Figure 5.2: Selection from possible entries

5.3   Overhead Costing Sheet

The overhead costing sheet method is commonly used to add additional cost to internal orders.

An overhead costing sheet can be added to the internal order master record.

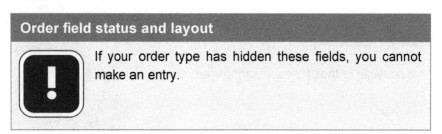

Order field status and layout

If your order type has hidden these fields, you cannot make an entry.

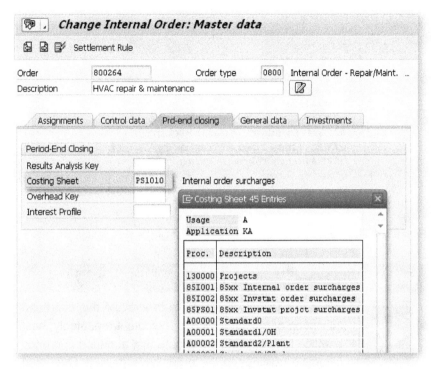

Figure 5.3: Enter costing sheet on order master record

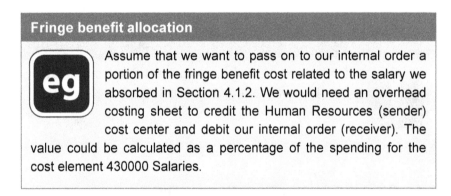

Fringe benefit allocation

Assume that we want to pass on to our internal order a portion of the fringe benefit cost related to the salary we absorbed in Section 4.1.2. We would need an overhead costing sheet to credit the Human Resources (sender) cost center and debit our internal order (receiver). The value could be calculated as a percentage of the spending for the cost element 430000 Salaries.

Executing the allocation is generally done as a batch job on a schedule during the period end close process.

The menu paths for individual and collective processing are shown in Figure 5.4.

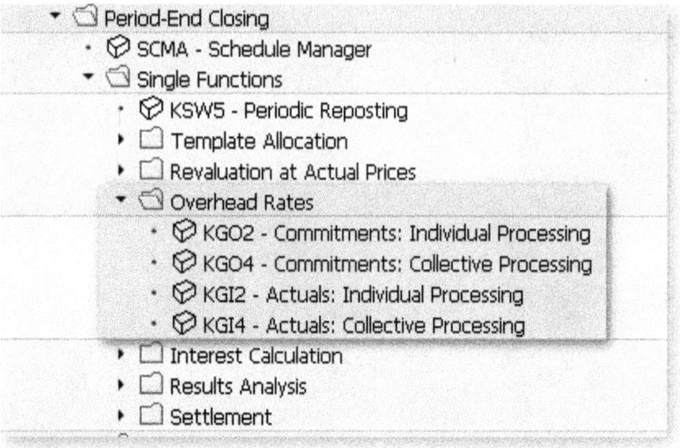

Period-End Closing
  · ♥ SCMA - Schedule Manager
  ▼ ⬒ Single Functions
    · ♥ KSW5 - Periodic Reposting
    ▸ ☐ Template Allocation
    ▸ ☐ Revaluation at Actual Prices
    ▼ ⬒ Overhead Rates
      · ♥ KGO2 - Commitments: Individual Processing
      · ♥ KGO4 - Commitments: Collective Processing
      · ♥ KGI2 - Actuals: Individual Processing
      · ♥ KGI4 - Actuals: Collective Processing
    ▸ ☐ Interest Calculation
    ▸ ☐ Results Analysis
    ▸ ☐ Settlement

Figure 5.4: Overhead rate menu

Periodicity

While it is technically possible to execute this overhead allocation at any time, and to execute it repeatedly, best practice is to execute the processing at period end once incoming postings to the order have ceased. Overhead calculations can be reversed.

Master data

If there is no overhead costing sheet on the order master data, there will be no calculation here.

5.4 Overhead Costing Sheet Customizing

Customizing of an overhead costing sheet involves three main components: the base, the rate, and the credit. Let's look at each component while applying our example.

Fringe benefit allocation

 Assume that we want to pass on to our internal order a portion of the fringe benefit cost related to the salary we absorbed in section 4.1.2. We would need an overhead costing sheet to credit the Human Resources (sender) cost center and debit our internal order (receiver). The value could be calculated as 21% percent of the spending for the cost element 430000 Salaries.

▶ Base defines the basis for the overhead calculation. It is defined by cost element and origin group.

CONTROLLING • INTERNAL ORDERS • ACTUAL POSTINGS • OVERHEAD RATES • COSTING SHEET: COMPONENTS • DEFINE CALCULATION BASES REFERRING TO COST ELEMENT AND ORIGIN KZB2

Select the NEW ENTRIES pushbutton.

Enter a four-character alphanumeric base and a name.

Press ⌈Enter⌉, select your row, and navigate to the details folder in the DIALOG STRUCTURE on the left of the screen, as seen in Figure 5.5.

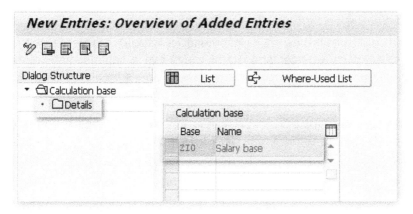

Figure 5.5: Calculation base

Enter/confirm the controlling area.

Select the NEW ENTRIES pushbutton.

In the NEW ENTRIES: OVERVIEW OF ADDED ENTRIES screen, enter the cost elements and optional origin group that the basis for the calculation comprises. Notice the radio buttons to restrict the base by total, fixed, or variable cost. Our example would appear this way: see Figure 5.6.

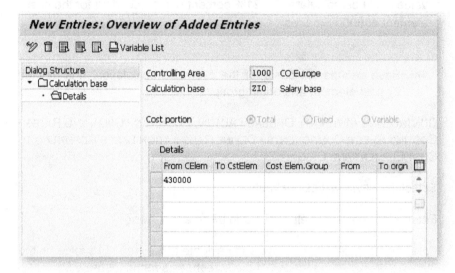

Figure 5.6: Cost element definition of base

▶ A rate defines how much overhead to calculate, expressed by a quantity or a percentage. Rates may have a dependency, i.e., a different rate by plant/company code/business area/etc. You may also distinguish between actual and plan rates.

CONTROLLING • INTERNAL ORDERS • ACTUAL POSTINGS • OVERHEAD RATES • COSTING SHEET: COMPONENTS • DEFINE PERCENTAGE OVERHEAD RATES KZZ2

Select the NEW ENTRIES pushbutton.

Enter a four-character alphanumeric O/H rate and a name.

Use the dropdown for dependency to select from the available options as seen in Figure 5.7. Our example will be the overhead type.

Different rate by dependency

To enter a different rate for plan versus actual, or a different rate by profit center or plant, etc., select the appropriate dependency from the dropdown.

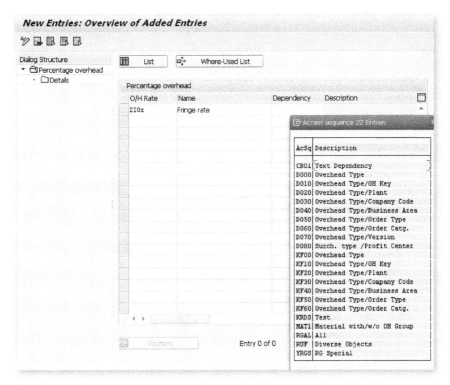

Figure 5.7: Rate dependency

Press Enter, select your row, and navigate to the details folder in the DIALOG STRUCTURE on the left of the screen as seen in Figure 5.8.

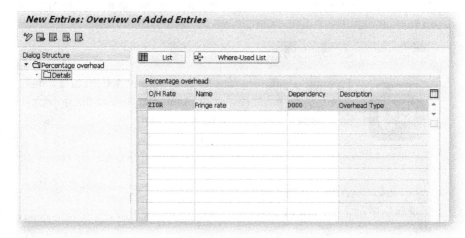

Figure 5.8: O/H Rate

Select the NEW ENTRIES pushbutton.

In the NEW ENTRIES: OVERVIEW OF ADDED ENTRIES screen, enter the validity period, controlling area, overhead type, and percentage. Our example would appear as in Figure 5.9.

New Entries: Overview of Added Entries

Dialog Structure
- Percentage overhead
  - Details

| O/H Rate | ZIOR | Fringe rate |
| Dependency | D000 | Overhead Type |

Details

Valid from	To	CO Area	Ovrhd type	Percentage	Unit
01/01/2016	12/31/2016	1000	1	21.000	%

Figure 5.9: O/H parameters

▶ Credit defines which cost object is the sender of the overhead, and which secondary cost element to use when posting.

CONTROLLING • INTERNAL ORDERS • ACTUAL POSTINGS • OVERHEAD RATES • COSTING SHEET: COMPONENTS • DEFINE CREDITS KZE2

Select the NEW ENTRIES pushbutton.

Enter a three-character alphanumeric O/H rate and a name.

Press ⌈Enter⌋, select your row, and navigate to the details folder in the DIALOG STRUCTURE on the left of the screen, as seen in Figure 5.10.

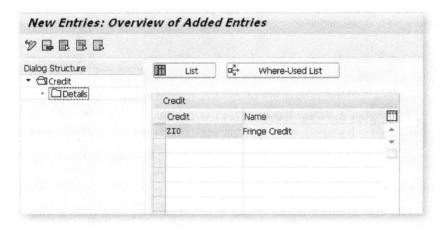

Figure 5.10: Credit entry

Enter/confirm the CONTROLLING AREA.

Select the NEW ENTRIES pushbutton.

In the NEW ENTRIES: OVERVIEW OF ADDED ENTRIES screen, enter the following: ending validity period, secondary cost element (must be category 41), optional origin group, optional fixed percentage, and one of the three cost objects of overhead cost controlling. Our example appears as in Figure 5.11.

New Entries: Overview of Added Entries

Dialog Structure	Controlling Area	1000	CO Europe				
▾ ☐ Credit	Credit	ZIO	Fringe Credit				
· ⬜ Details							

Details

Valid to	Cost Elem.	OrGp	Fxd %	Cost Center	Order	Business Process
12/31/2016	655200		*	2200		

Figure 5.11: Credit definition

Fixed %

If the field is left blank, the system will return an asterisk (*). When the overhead is posted, the fixed portion will be assigned based on how the sender cost center was planned. For most manufacturing organizations, the fixed cost portion is quite important and may be provided to you by cost accountants for entry here.

Now that we have created our three costing sheet components, it is time to assign them to an overhead costing sheet.

Variant principle

Each component created can be assigned to multiple overhead costing sheets. Within the costing sheet, the component may have distinct values assigned.

▶ Overhead Costing Sheet: Here we bring together various components to create a calculation.

CONTROLLING • INTERNAL ORDERS • ACTUAL POSTINGS • OVERHEAD RATES • MAINTAIN CALCULATION PROCEDURES KZS2

Select the NEW ENTRIES pushbutton.

Enter a six-character alphanumeric costing sheet and a description.

Press Enter, select your row, and navigate to costing sheet rows in the DIALOG STRUCTURE as seen in Figure 5.12.

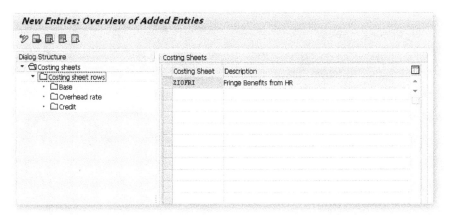

Figure 5.12: Costing sheet description

Select the NEW ENTRIES pushbutton.

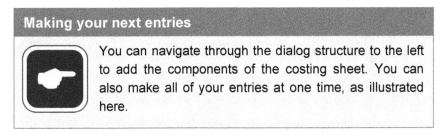

Making your next entries

You can navigate through the dialog structure to the left to add the components of the costing sheet. You can also make all of your entries at one time, as illustrated here.

Think of the structure of the costing sheet as an equation.

First, we need to define the basis for the calculation, ZIO Salary Base.

Next we need to indicate how to perform the calculation, ZIOR Fringe Rate.

Lastly, we need to indicate which cost object is the sender of the overhead, ZIO Fringe Credit.

The receiver will be the cost object whose master data contains this overhead costing sheet.

In Figure 5.13, we can see how these values are used to create the costing sheet rows:

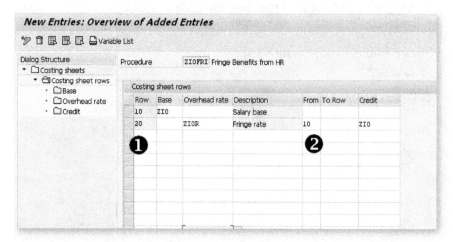

Figure 5.13: Costing sheet rows

As seen in Figure 5.13 above, the rows ❶ structure the calculation. When we want to apply an overhead rate to a previously entered base, use the from and to row columns ❷.

This mathematical equation is represented here:

Calculate the basis for the overhead using Z10 (cost element 430000) x the overhead rate of ZIOR (21% for actual costs) = result.

When posting the result, reference the credit ZIO (cost center 2200, secondary cost element 655200.

This is a very simple example of using an overhead costing sheet. The costing sheet could contain multiple sets of calculations, i.e., more rows of base, rate, and credit.

Assignment to master data

Each participating cost object can have only one overhead costing sheet assignment.

5.5 Settlement

Settlement is the most common method of overhead allocation from internal orders. During this periodic process, the costs accumulated on the internal order are transferred to the appropriate receivers.

Periodicity

While it is technically possible to execute settlement at any time, and to execute it repeatedly, a best practice is to execute the processing at period end, once incoming postings to the order have ceased. Settlement can be reversed and re-executed.

Each internal order must contain settings that indicate how settlement will be executed. There are two methods of assigning these settings:

Settlement to one receiver

On each internal order master record, the period end closing tab allows entry of a single cost center and secondary cost element for the settlement posting, as seen in Figure 5.14. Once an entry is made here, the features of the settlement rule pushbutton are disabled. Since extended settlement is a far more flexible method, it is more widely used—even in cases of one receiver.

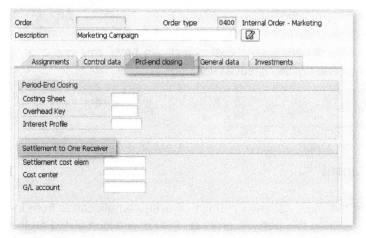

Figure 5.14: Period End Close tab of an order

Field status and screen layout

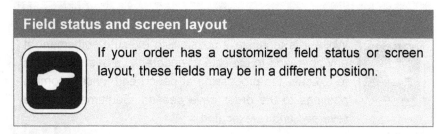

If your order has a customized field status or screen layout, these fields may be in a different position.

Cost element for settlement

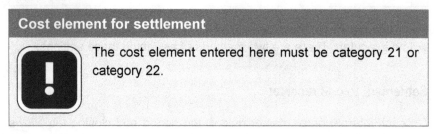

The cost element entered here must be category 21 or category 22.

Extended settlement

Extended settlement, as seen in Figure 5.15, can allow multiple receivers of various types, as well as flexible options for distributing the cost. You can also use validity periods to end and begin a new settlement rule or rules. The benefits of this method are:

▶ Flexible assignment of receiver object(s) ❶.

▶ Distribution to receiver objects by percentage ❷, equivalence numbers, or specific amounts.

- ▶ Validity period of each rule ❸.
- ▶ History of rule usage ❹.

A settlement profile assigned to the order type determines which options are allowed. To view which profile is assigned to the order, from the MAINTAIN SETTLEMENT RULE: OVERVIEW screen, select GO TO • SETTLEMENT PARAMETERS.

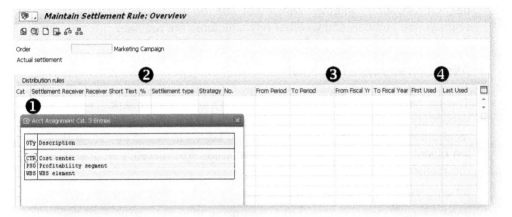

Figure 5.15: Extended settlement

As seen in Figure 5.16, we can now identify the settlement parameters assigned by the order type.

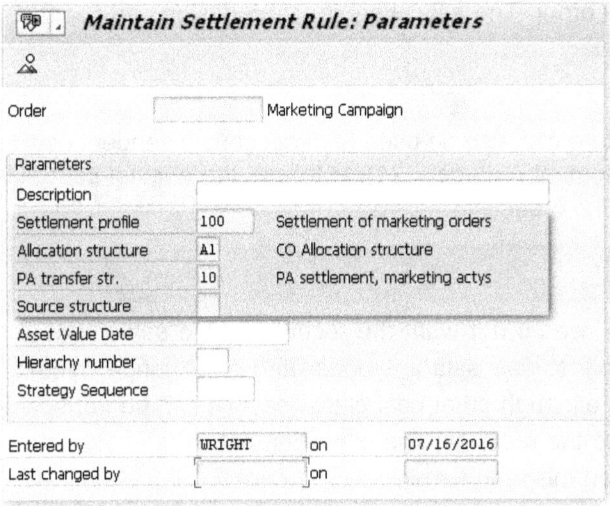

Figure 5.16: Maintain settlement rule parameters

Let's review the purpose of each profile and structure seen in Figure 5.16:

Settlement profile (required)

The settlement profile determines how many distribution rules you can enter on the order; which objects you can settle to (e.g., cost center, order, GL account); whether settlement can be by percentage-amount-equivalence number; and whether any structures are required.

Allocation structure (optional)

The allocation structure determines whether settlement will post using a secondary cost element (category 21) or using the original cost element as charged to the order. This decision can be made based on the receiving object. This is an important decision when transparency of cost is a requirement.

Receiver transparency

 Often, we want the receiving cost center to have a fully transparent view of the way the cost was classified as it was charged to the order. At the same time, we may not want to show those details if the receiver is another internal order. The allocation structure design can support this requirement.

The allocation structure can also be used to direct certain sender costs to a secondary cost element (category 21) or to use the original cost element as charged to the order.

Sensitive information

 Often, we do not want the receiver of the settlement to be able to see salary, wages, and other fringe benefit costs although other cost classifications can be transparent to the receiver. The allocation structure design can support this requirement.

PA transfer structure (optional)

If cost based profitability analysis (CO-PA) is in scope and you settle to profitability segments, this structure determines the value fields for posting.

Source structure (optional)

The source structure allows the distribution (settlement) rule to assign certain costs to specific receivers. If it is in scope, the extended settlement screen will have an additional column, as seen in Figure 5.17.

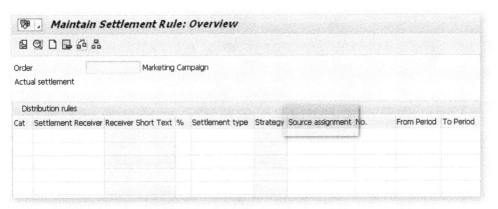

Figure 5.17: Source structure

Benefits of a source structure

We have these spending classifications: External Purchases (source U11) and Internal Labor Cost (source U12). We want to settle External Purchases to cost center 1000 and Internal Labor Cost to a different cost center, 2200. Our settlement rule would appear as in Figure 5.18. At settlement, the value flow would reflect this rule.

Maintain Settlement Rule: Overview

Order [_____] Marketing Campaign

Actual settlement

Distribution rules

Cat	Settlement Receiver	Receiver Short Text	%	Settlement type	Strategy	Source assignment	No.	Fron
CTR	1000	Corporate Services	10...	PER		U11	1	
CTR	2200	Human Resources	10...	PER		U12	2	

Figure 5.18: Settlement rule with source structure

As part of the period-end closing process, order settlement is executed. The following transactions can be used:

ACCOUNTING • CONTROLLING • INTERNAL ORDERS • PERIOD-END CLOSING • SINGLE FUNCTIONS • SETTLEMENT • INDIVIDUAL PROCESSING KO88

ACCOUNTING • CONTROLLING • INTERNAL ORDERS • PERIOD-END CLOSING • SINGLE FUNCTIONS • SETTLEMENT • COLLECTIVE PROCESSING KOG8

Generally, the collective processing transaction is executed using background processing on a schedule determined by Finance during the period-end closing.

In our business process review, we will execute KO88 and examine the output.

 Now that we have an understanding of the available options for settlement, let's return to our business process example.

Our training event has been completed, and it is Period End Close. We need to allocate the cost of the event to the cost centers whose employees attended the training. Those cost centers are 1000 Corporate Services, 2300 Purchasing, and 420SHIP Shipping Admin. The decision has been made to share the cost evenly among these cost centers.

To maintain the internal order settlement rule, use either of these transactions:

ORDER MANAGER KO04

CHANGE KO02

Enter the order number.

In Change Mode, select the SETTLEMENT RULE pushbutton Settlement Rule .

Our data entry would look like the one seen in Figure 5.19. Notice that we could allocate to the receivers by a percentage, equivalence numbers, or absolute amount(s). By entering the equivalence number 1 in each row, each of the three receivers will get one third of the cost (1/[1+1+1]).

Figure 5.19: Create settlement rule

How do changes in settlement profiles affect existing orders?

Generally, when changes are made in customizing to settlement profiles or other changes are made to order types, the change is effective for new orders created from that point forward. Customizing changes to settlement profiles are not retroactive.

Now that our order contains a settlement rule, we can complete the period end settlement.

There are two transactions available for order settlement:

ACCOUNTING • CONTROLLING • INTERNAL ORDERS • PERIOD-END CLOSING • SINGLE FUNCTIONS • SETTLEMENT • INDIVIDUAL PROCESSING KO88

and

ACCOUNTING • CONTROLLING • INTERNAL ORDERS • PERIOD-END CLOSING • SINGLE FUNCTIONS • SETTLEMENT • COLLECTIVE PROCESSING KOG8

Generally, KOG8 is preferred and is executed as a background job throughout the closing process. KOG8 also provides a selection variant to settle like orders together.

For our example, we will enter the parameters in KO88 as seen in Figure 5.20. Notice that the settlement could be posted in a different posting period, as long as that period is in the same fiscal year. This is useful if we are attempting to settle order balances from a previous posting period in the current period. Also notice the test run checkbox, which is useful in simulations.

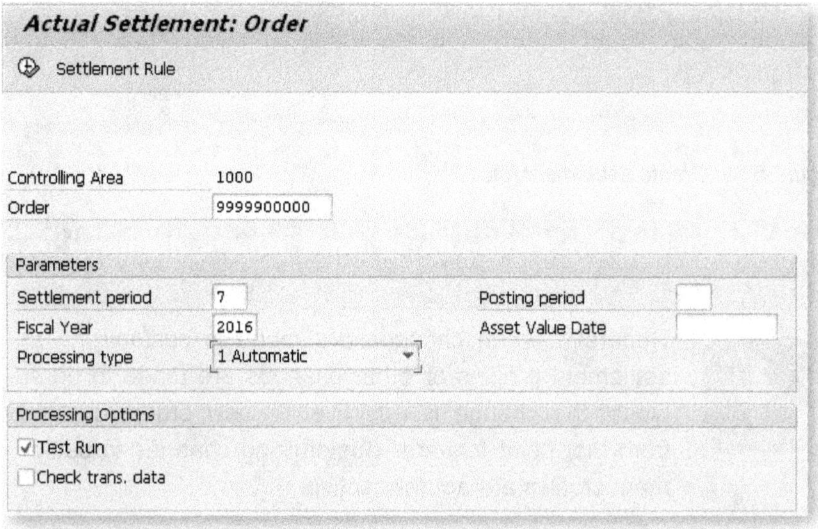

Actual Settlement: Order

Settlement Rule

Controlling Area	1000
Order	9999900000

Parameters

Settlement period	7	Posting period	
Fiscal Year	2016	Asset Value Date	
Processing type	1 Automatic		

Processing Options

☑ Test Run
☐ Check trans. data

Figure 5.20: KO88 Settlement parameters

After removing the test run check box and executing settlement, the system returns a RESULT list, as seen in Figure 5.21. From here, select the DETAILS LIST icon.

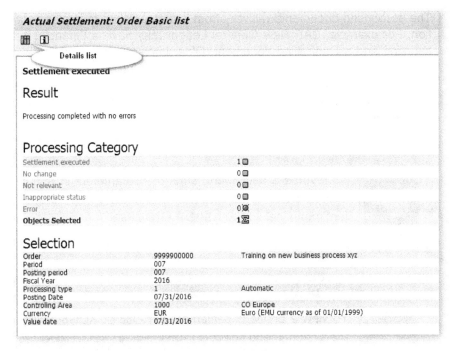

Figure 5.21: Order settlement result with details list

As seen in Figure 5.22, on the DETAILS LIST-SETTLED VALUES screen, the sender and receivers are identified, as well as the receiver values ❶. There are also pushbuttons to see details about the sender and receiver line items and the accounting documents, a toggle to the order master record and settlement rule, and a report-to-report interface ❷.

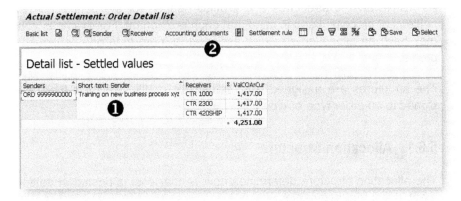

Figure 5.22: Order details list

The accounting documents will vary from implementation to implementation. For example, SAP New General Ledger may have a Financial Accounting and a Controlling document. Older implementations may have only a Controlling document. Also, the allocation structure may post using either the original cost elements or secondary cost elements. At a minimum, you should see the sender object allocating the overhead to the receiver object(s) as per the settlement rule.

Settlement reversal

 To reverse a settlement, enter the parameters in KO88 or KOG8 exactly as they were executed. Using the system menu, select SETTLEMENT • REVERSE.

Previous settlement

 To view a previous settlement in KO88 or KOG8, using the system menu select GO TO • PREVIOUS SETTLEMENT.

5.6 Settlement Customizing

As we review the structures and profiles needed for the periodic order settlement process, keep in mind that each is a variant. For example, you may have an allocation structure assigned to more than one settlement profile.

The structures are assigned to a settlement profile, which is then assigned to an order type or types.

5.6.1 Allocation Structure

The allocation structure determines how sender cost is posted at settlement. It is a required setting.

This design may be quite simple: All sender values could post via a secondary cost element at settlement.

This design may be quite complicated: Sender values for salary and wages should post via the original cost elements when settlement is to a cost center, but they should post to a single secondary cost element when settlement is to an order.

The design will be built around transparency and the reporting requirement. In some cases, we don't need to be transparent to the sender. Each organization—and in fact, each order type—may have a different requirement.

 From our business process example, the requirement is to provide as much transparency as possible to the receiver cost centers. We need an allocation structure to support this requirement.

To create an allocation structure from the IMG menu:

CONTROLLING • INTERNAL ORDERS • ACTUAL POSTINGS • SETTLEMENT • MAINTAIN ALLOCATION STRUCTURES OKO6

Select the NEW ENTRIES pushbutton.

Enter a two-character alphanumeric ALLOCATION STRUCTURE and a DESCRIPTION.

Press ⌈Enter⌋ and select your row, then navigate to the ASSIGNMENTS folder in the DIALOG STRUCTURE on the left of the screen.

> **Purpose of assignments**
>
> In a next step, we will assign cost elements to define the assignment created here. Assignments are used to segregate the sender's posted amounts by cost element. This is necessary if you want to later post the settlement of various assignments on different cost elements.

Select the NEW ENTRIES pushbutton.

Enter a three-character alphanumeric ASSIGNMENT and a TEXT.

Press ⌈Enter⌋ and select your row, then navigate to the SOURCE folder in the DIALOG STRUCTURE at the left of the screen.

In the Change View: Source Details screen, enter the cost elements that the assignment comprises. Note that a single, range, or group of cost elements can be entered, as seen in Figure 5.23.

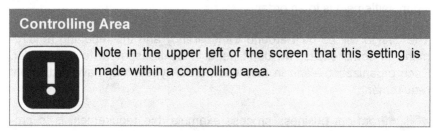

Navigate to the SETTLEMENT COST ELEMENTS folder in the DIALOG STRUCTURE on the left of the screen.

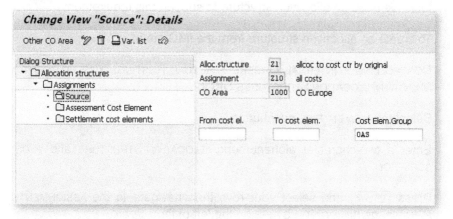

Figure 5.23: Define source cost elements

Navigate to the SETTLEMENT COST ELEMENTS folder in the DIALOG STRUC-TURE on the left of the screen.

Select the NEW ENTRIES pushbutton.

As seen in Figure 5.24, the settlement cost elements section requires three entries:

❶ The receiver category, e.g., cost center, order, etc.

❷ A checkbox for by cost element. Selecting this box means settlement to the indicated receiver type will post on the original cost elements.

❸ The settlement cost element, which must be a secondary cost element with category 21 or category 22 on its master record. An entry here means settlement to the indicated receiver will post on this cost element.

> ## Original or settlement cost element
>
> ![!] You cannot set both indicators for the same receiver category.

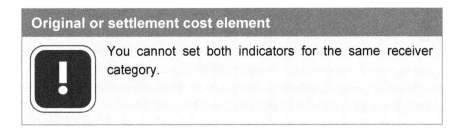

Figure 5.24: Settlement cost elements

Since our requirement is to settle to cost centers with transparency, your entry would appear as seen in Figure 5.25.

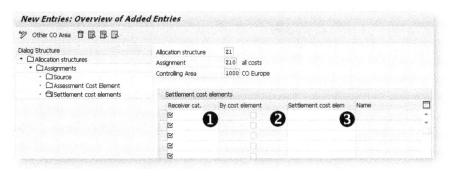

Figure 5.25: Settlement cost elements as per requirements

The allocation structure must be assigned to an order type. We will take this step later on.

Overlap of cost elements

 Within an allocation structure, it is possible to include a cost element in multiple source assignments. If this occurs, the system will return an error when settlement is executed. It is a good practice to check the assignments tab once all sources have been entered. There is an overlapping check indicator here with a green/yellow/red light. As seen in Figure 5.26, the light should always be green.

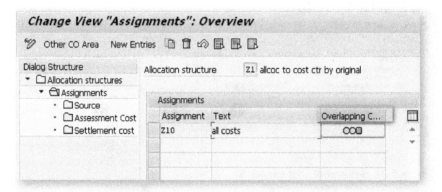

Figure 5.26: Overlapping check indicator

5.6.2   Source Structure

The source structure allows the dissection of sender values so different types of cost can have their own rule in the settlement. It is an optional setting.

For example, salary and wages should always settle to a cost center, while all other spending should settle to another internal order.

To create a source structure from the IMG menu:

CONTROLLING • INTERNAL ORDERS • ACTUAL POSTINGS • SETTLEMENT • MAINTAIN SOURCE STRUCTURE OKEU

Create the ASSIGNMENTS and identify the SOURCE as in section 5.6.1.

Controlling Area

Note in the upper left of the screen that this setting is made within a controlling area.

5.6.3 PA Transfer Structure

When cost-based profitability analysis (CO-PA) is in scope, settlement may occur to its profitably segments. Because CO-PA analyzes value by value field rather than cost element, you must provide a mapping from the settlement cost element(s) to the value fields.

To create a PA Transfer structure from the IMG menu:

CONTROLLING • INTERNAL ORDERS • ACTUAL POSTINGS • SETTLEMENT • MAINTAIN PA TRANSFER STRUCTURE KEI1

Create the ASSIGNMENTS and identify the SOURCE as in section 5.6.1.

On each SOURCE DETAIL, select the costs/revenue radio button.

As seen in Figure 5.27, on the value fields tab indicate quantity or value field ❶; whether the value should be treated as fixed, variable or total cost ❷; and which value field to post to ❸.

Figure 5.27: PA transfer structure value field assignment

115

Controlling Area

Note that in each screen, this setting is made within a controlling area. The system derives the operating concern on the PA transfer structure from this controlling area.

5.6.4 Settlement Profile

The settlement profile brings together previous structures and contains other important settings. It is assigned to the order type. To participate in the settlement process, an order must have a settlement profile.

In Figure 5.28 below, you can view the new entries screen to create a settlement profile. Here is the purpose of each setting:

Actual Costs/Cost of Sales

This setting controls the messages sent if orders contain a balance when an attempt is made to change the status to closed or delete.

- ▶ To be settled in full: If the order has a balance, the system will return an error message if you attempt to set the order status to closed or delete. This ensures that all costs are settled before closing or deleting the order. This is the default setting.

- ▶ Can be settled: If the order has a balance, the system will return a warning message if you attempt to set the order status to closed or delete.

- ▶ Not for settlement: if the order has a balance, the system will not return a message if you attempt to set the order status to closed or delete.

Radio button

This is a single choice. The default setting is 'to be settled in full.' Make changes to this only in special cases.

Default values

▶ Structures: Here you can assign the three structures as defaults. The allocation structure will be required at settlement. The other two are optional, as mentioned earlier.

▶ Default object type: Assign a cost object type as the default for the settlement rule.

Indicators

▶ 100% validation: If selected, the system will check that the total does not exceed 100% when percentage settlement rules are entered on the order. An information message will be returned to the user. The distribution must be corrected before settlement or the order will not be settled. This validation also works when equivalence numbers, rather than percentages, are used.

▶ % settlement: Displays a column in the settlement rule for the user to enter a percentage.

▶ Equivalence numbers: Displays a column in the settlement rule for the user to enter an equivalence number.

▶ Amount settlement: Displays a column in the settlement rule for the user to enter an amount.

▶ Variances to costing-based CO-PA: This setting is used with production/process orders to create a posting to CO-PA.

Valid receivers

This setting controls what users see in the settlement rule dropdown for receiver object types. Generally, the not allowed option is assigned to receiver object types not in scope.

From this list of possible settlement receivers, assign one of three settings: not allowed, required, or optional.

Other parameters

▶ Document type: Specify a document type for postings to Financial Accounting (optional).

▶ Max. no.dist. rls: The settlement rule will display this many lines for entry.

▶ Residence time: Controls how many calendar months the settlement documents can be retained. The system will default to three months, if left blank.

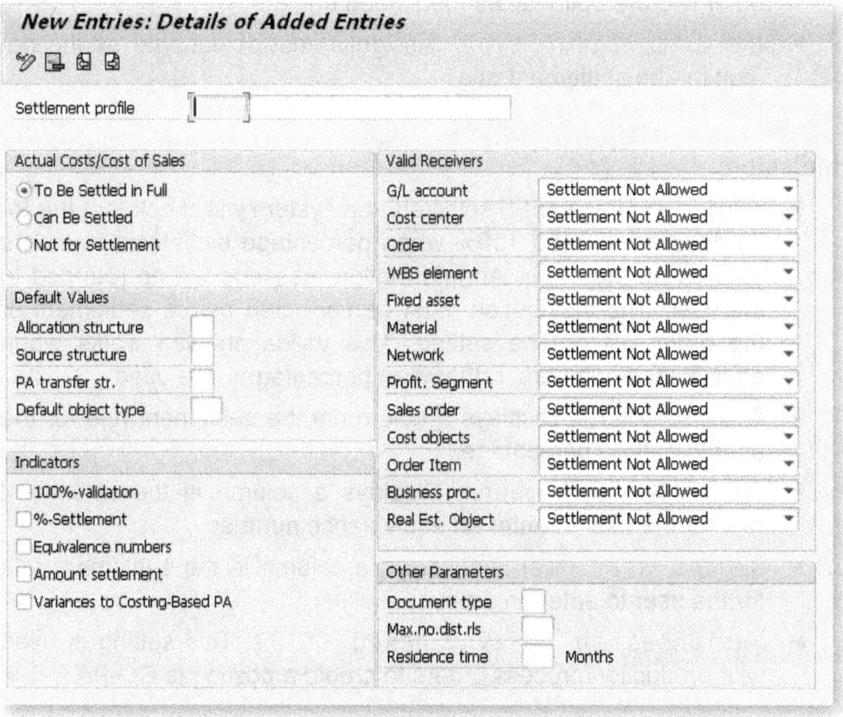

Figure 5.28: Detail of settlement profile

From our business process example, we need a settlement profile that allows transparent settlement to cost centers. Previously, we created an allocation structure for this requirement. Now let's create the profile and assign it to our previously created order type.

To create a settlement profile from the IMG menu:

CONTROLLING • INTERNAL ORDERS • ACTUAL POSTINGS • SETTLEMENT • MAINTAIN SETTLEMENT PROFILES OKO7

In the SELECT ACTIVITY dialog, choose MAINTAIN SETTLEMENT PROFILES.

Select the NEW ENTRIES pushbutton.

Enter a six-character alphanumeric SETTLEMENT PROFILE and a DESCRIPTION.

Make the appropriate selections to support the requirement.

Allow for future requirements

Notice I have selected percent, equivalent, and amount settlement, and have provided ten distribution rules. This gives some flexibility to the user going forward, without requiring change requests.

The settlement profile should be as seen in Figure 5.29.

New Entries: Details of Added Entries

Settlement profile   ZIO1   Profile for settlement to cctr

Actual Costs/Cost of Sales		Valid Receivers	
● To Be Settled in Full		G/L account	Settlement Not Allowed ▼
○ Can Be Settled		Cost center	2 Settlement Required ▼
○ Not for Settlement		Order	Settlement Not Allowed ▼
		WBS element	Settlement Not Allowed ▼
Default Values		Fixed asset	Settlement Not Allowed ▼
Allocation structure	Z1 allcoc to cost...	Material	Settlement Not Allowed ▼
Source structure		Network	Settlement Not Allowed ▼
PA transfer str.		Profit. Segment	Settlement Not Allowed ▼
Default object type		Sales order	Settlement Not Allowed ▼
		Cost objects	Settlement Not Allowed ▼
Indicators		Order Item	Settlement Not Allowed ▼
✓ 100%-validation		Business proc.	Settlement Not Allowed ▼
✓ %-Settlement		Real Est. Object	Settlement Not Allowed ▼
✓ Equivalence numbers			
✓ Amount settlement		**Other Parameters**	
☐ Variances to Costing-Based PA		Document type	
		Max.no.dist.rls	10
		Residence time	3 Months

Figure 5.29: Completed settlement profile

Green arrow **back twice** to the SELECT ACTIVITY dialog and select ENTER SETTLEMENT PROFILE IN ORDER TYPES.

Position to your order type and enter the settlement profile as seen in Figure 5.30.

119

Change View "Order Types": Overview

New Entries

Order Types

Cat	Name	Cat	Settlement profile
WF01	Internal Order: Demo Workflow	1	20
Z18	m wright test copy from 0800	1	40
Z400	Internal Order - Marketing	1	Z1
Z600	Internal Order - Capital Spending	1	50
ZEBP	Internal Order - Production	1	30
ZIAS	Cap. Investments - Line items/Comp. 1000	1	IAS
ZIO1	Training event to cost centers	1	ZIO1
ZMW	m wright test	1	40

Figure 5.30: Assign settlement profile to order type

The user impact of our settings is seen in the settlement rule of an order created with order type ZIO1 as seen in Figure 5.31

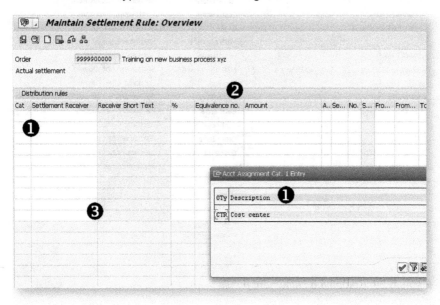

Figure 5.31: Order settlement rule

❶ From the category dropdown, cost center is the only available selection.

❷ Users can enter the allocation as a percent, equivalence number, or amount.

❸ There are ten rows to enter settlement rules.

5.6.5   Selection Variant for Settlement

Here, we can create variants for use on the application menu in the collective processing transaction KOG8. Because order numbers are sequentially added using the assigned number range, the use of selection variants is a good way to limit which orders are processed.

To create a selection variant for settlement from the IMG menu:

CONTROLLING • INTERNAL ORDERS • ACTUAL POSTINGS • SETTLEMENT • DEFINE SELECTION VARIANTS FOR SETTLEMENT

5.6.6   Automatic Generation of Settlement Rule

Here, we can create a strategy to use a field from the internal order master record in creation of a settlement rule automatically. SAP supplies standard strategies for settlement to many receivers, including profitability segment, responsible cost center, requesting cost center, and WBS element.

To create the strategy and assign it to an order type from the IMG menu:

CONTROLLING • INTERNAL ORDERS • ACTUAL POSTINGS • SETTLEMENT • AUTOMATIC GENERATION OF SETTLEMENT RULES

6 Reporting

SAP delivers hundreds of standard reports for use in analyzing internal orders. In this chapter, we will review some of the most popular reports in the SAP system.

6.1 User settings

This setting allows us to create default values for many of the reporting selection parameters. If you execute these reports on a regular basis, this is a great efficiency tool.

To create user settings from the SAP Easy Access Menu:

ACCOUNTING • CONTROLLING • INTERNAL ORDERS • INFORMATION SYSTEM • USER SETTINGS RPO0

As seen in Figure 6.1, defaults for controlling area, order groups, planning and reporting periods, as well as currency, can be made here.

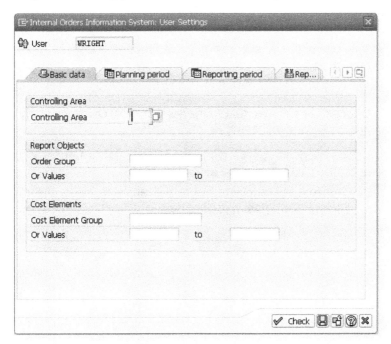

Figure 6.1: User settings RPO0

6.2 Information System

The information system menu groups reports by their purpose. As seen in Figure 6.2, there are several comparison groups, planning, line item, and master data reports.

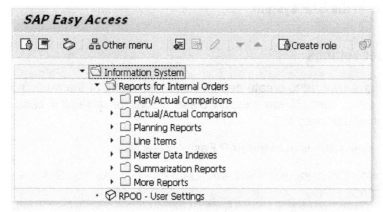

Figure 6.2: Order Information System menu

6.2.1 Report execution

Let's begin with one of the most commonly used reports, a comparison of actual and plan costs.

CONTROLLING • INTERNAL ORDERS • INFORMATION SYSTEM • REPORTS FOR INTERNAL ORDERS • PLAN/ACTUAL COMPARISONS • ORDERS: ACTU-AL/PLAN/VARIANCE S_ALR_87012993

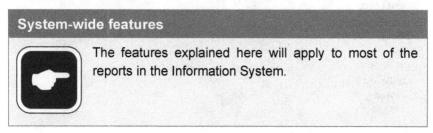

System-wide features

The features explained here will apply to most of the reports in the Information System.

As seen in Figure 6.3, we can enter various parameters for report execution.

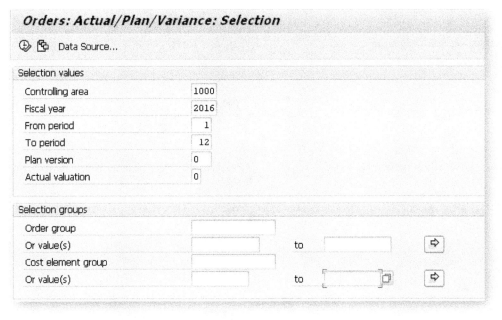

Figure 6.3: Order report selection parameters

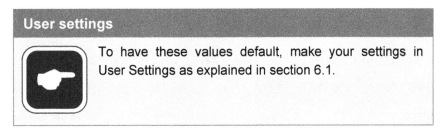

User settings

To have these values default, make your settings in User Settings as explained in section 6.1.

To activate expert mode from the parameter selection screen, navigate to ENVIRONMENT • OPTIONS and select the `expert mode` checkbox as seen in Figure 6.4.

Figure 6.4: Activate expert mode

Once expert mode has been activated, there are additional features available above the SELECTION VALUES group box, as seen in Figure 6.5.

▶ Variation. In addition to any variation in the report, you can see different levels of detail by selecting explode, single value, or do not explode.

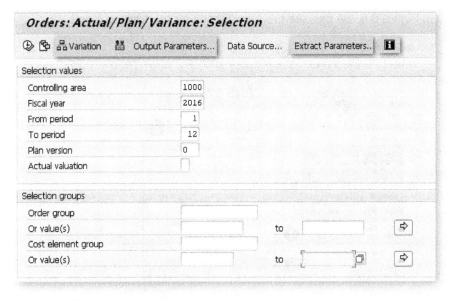

Figure 6.5: Expert mode additional features

▶ Currency translation. Key figures in the report can be translated to different currencies.

▶ Output parameters. When exiting the report, you can add the option to create an extract of the data.

▶ Extract parameters. Further defines the extract, including features to manage extracts such as an expiration date.

▶ Information. Help on the report group

To execute the report, enter the values in the Selection values group box, and the order group or single, range, or list of orders in the Selection groups' group box. Note that a cost element group, etc. can be entered to further define the report.

In Figure 6.6, we can see the report result for our training event.

Orders: Actual/Plan/Variance ❻

Cost elements	Actual	Plan	Abs. var.	Var.(%)
430000 Salaries - base wages	200.00		200.00	
476900 Miscellaneous costs	250.00	200.00	50.00	25.00
477050 Instructor Fees	2,301.00	2,500.00	199.00-	7.96-
477055 Training Material	1,500.00	500.00	1,000.00	200.00
* Costs	4,251.00	3,200.00	1,051.00	32.84
430000 Salaries - base wages	200.00-		200.00-	
476900 Miscellaneous costs	250.00-		250.00-	
477050 Instructor Fees	2,301.00-		2,301.00-	
477055 Training Material	1,500.00-		1,500.00-	
* Settled costs	4,251.00-		4,251.00-	
** Balance		3,200.00	3,200.00-	100.00-

Orders: Actual/Plan/Variance — Date: 07/19/2016 04:31:01 — Page: 2 / 2

Order/Group ❶ 9999900000 Training on new business process xyz
Reporting period 1 ~ 12 2016

Figure 6.6: Report result

In Figure 6.6 the order number and description are displayed in the report header ❶. The actual, plan, and variance amounts are in the columns of the report, sorted by cost element ❷. The total actual and planned costs are summed up ❸, the total values settled are summed up ❹, and the order balance is displayed ❺.

Our order has completed the settlement process so the order balance is zero ("null" here), but we can see how the monies were spent, as well as how they were allocated elsewhere.

Settlement cost element

In the settled cost section of the report, the cost element named in the settlement profile will be displayed. Our settlement profile provided transparency by posting settlement on the original cost elements.

Also in Figure 6.6, note the function icons at the top of the report ❻. Expert mode added functions here such as export report, presentation graphics, currency translation, and threshold definitions.

Report refresh

One of the best features of expert mode is the ability to refresh the report data without re-execution. Within the report, from the System Menu select REPORT • REFRESH.

To execute other reports from within this one, select the CALL UP REPORT icon ▦.

As seen in Figure 6.7, a list of available reports to select from will be displayed.

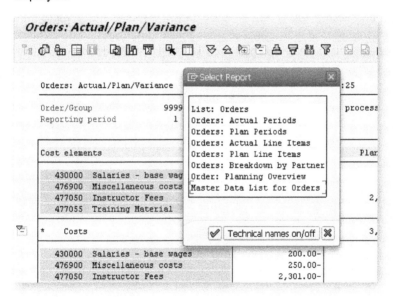

Figure 6.7: Call up report selection

6.2.2   Viewing line item detail

One of the favorite features of these types of reports is that they enable the user to review the line item details and associated FI-CO postings from within the report. By double-clicking on any line item, the select report list will display. Next, select the ORDERS: ACTUAL LINE ITEMS report to see details similar to those in Figure 6.8. Use the change layout series of icons ❶ to bring other fields into the view and structure the layout to meet your requirements.

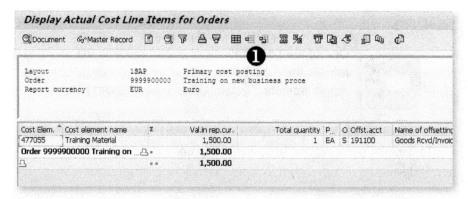

Figure 6.8: Orders: Actual line items

From the line item display, double-click an entry to see the original document. In Figure 6.9, you can see that the original document was the goods receipt to our purchase order. To see the FI-CO documents, select the FI Documents pushbutton.

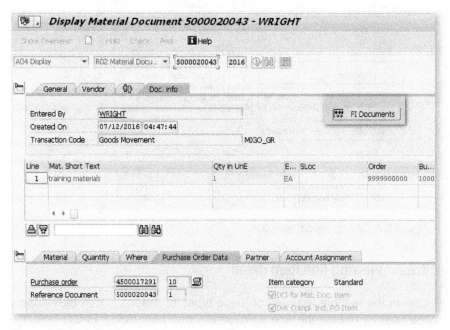

Figure 6.9: Material document

By selecting the accounting documents, we can review the financial posting, as seen in Figure 6.10.

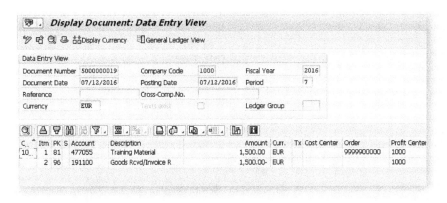

Figure 6.10: Financial accounting document

6.2.3 Other useful reports

For a list of order actual/plan balances, as seen in Figure 6.11, using an order group:

CONTROLLING • INTERNAL ORDERS • INFORMATION SYSTEM • REPORTS FOR INTERNAL ORDERS • PLAN/ACTUAL COMPARISONS • LIST: ORDERS S_ALR_ 87012995

List: orders

List: orders		Date: 07/19/2016 05:24:40			Page: 2 / 2
Order/Group	MYORDERS	My Orders			
Cost element group	*	Cost element group			
Reporting period	1 - 12 2016				

Orders	Actual	Plan	Abs. var.	Var.(%)
400297 Ad Campaign	500		500	
9999900000 Training on new business p		3,200	3,200-	100.00-
* Total	500	3,200	2,700-	84.38-

Figure 6.11: List: Orders S_ALR_87012995

For order actual spending by quarter, as seen in Figure 6.12

CONTROLLING • INTERNAL ORDERS • INFORMATION SYSTEM • REPORTS FOR INTERNAL ORDERS • ACTUAL/ACTUAL COMPARISONS • ORDERS: QUARTERLY COMPARISON – ACTUAL S_ALR_87013002 -

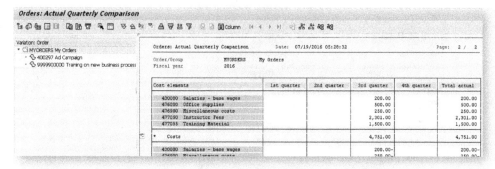

Figure 6.12: Orders: Actual Quarterly Comparison S_ALR_87013002

Variation

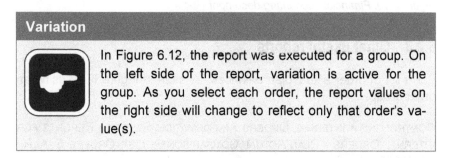

In Figure 6.12, the report was executed for a group. On the left side of the report, variation is active for the group. As you select each order, the report values on the right side will change to reflect only that order's value(s).

To get a listing of order master data using a selection variant (see Selection Variant) as seen in Figure 6.13:

CONTROLLING • INTERNAL ORDERS • INFORMATION SYSTEM • REPORTS FOR INTERNAL ORDERS • MASTER DATA INDEXES • INTERNAL ORDERS KOK5

Display Internal Order: Standard one-line

Order Master Data |◀ ◀ ▶ ▶| 🖨 ▽ ▽ ∑ 🗐 🗐   🖺 🖺Select   🖺Save   🗘

Order	Type	C	RefOrder	Entered by	Created on	Changed by	ChangeDate	Description
$$-WF01	$$	3		ROMAHN	08/31/1998			Musterauftag für Workflow
$0100	$$	3		SAP*	06/24/1992	NAGY	09/29/1995	Sample Order For Developm
$0400	$$	3		RADON	11/08/1994	WRIGHT	07/06/2016	Marketing Campaign
$0600	$$	3		RADON	11/08/1994	AUERT	11/30/1994	Capital spending order
$0601	$$	3	$0600	KIM	05/16/2001			Capital spending order
$0650	$$	3		MACHIELS	06/01/1995	HARTMANNJ	02/20/2003	
$0660	$$	3	$0650	ZIMMERMANNV	06/14/1996			
$0670	$$	3		ZIMMERMANNV	06/26/1996	ZIMMERMANNV	07/04/1996	

Figure 6.13: Master Data Indexes KOK5

Interactive report

 Double-click on an order to view the master record.

There are many other useful reports delivered by SAP in the Information System menu. The time it takes to review these reports is time very well spent.

6.3 Summarization Tools

Since internal orders have no standard hierarchy, and since the order master data design can vary widely thanks to the flexibility of order type configuration: it can be a challenge to capture the right data from the right orders in a report.

Summarization tools in the information system help with this challenge. By using a summarization hierarchy, we can execute a report of the master data fields and values in a hierarchical structure of our own design. The reporting output is interactive, with a link to a detailed cost report for the internal order.

To execute a report using summarization, from the SAP Easy Access Menu:

CONTROLLING • INTERNAL ORDERS • INFORMATION SYSTEM • TOOLS • SUMMARIZATION **KKRC**

The CO SUMMARIZATION will display as seen in Figure 6.14

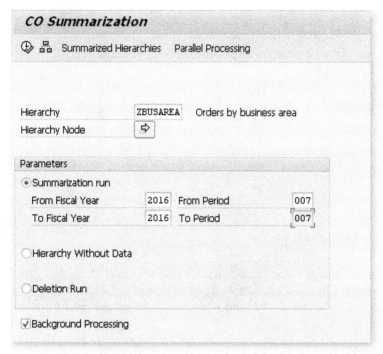

Figure 6.14: Summarization parameters

- ▶ Hierarchy. Enter the identification of the hierarchy to execute.
- ▶ Summarization run. Enter the years and periods to execute.
- ▶ Hierarchy without data. This will execute as a test run.
- ▶ Deletion run. This will delete all data from an existing hierarchy.
- ▶ Background processing. De-select to execute in the foreground.

Enter your selection parameters, and execute the transaction.

Upon completion, a log will be displayed as seen in Figure 6.15.

Return to the previous menu.

Now that the hierarchy has been populated with data, we can execute the report.

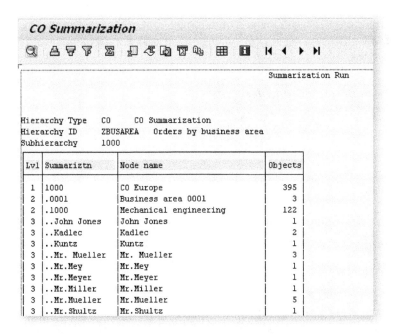

Figure 6.15: Summarization log

Select the hierarchy icon as seen in Figure 6.16.

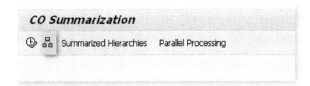

Figure 6.16: Hierarchy icon

What about existing data?

To view and select hierarchies that are already summarized, select the SUMMARIZED HIERARCHIES pushbutton.

As seen in Figure 6.17, the initial execution will not contain a layout. The hierarchy will display a folder for (in this example) each business area that has orders.

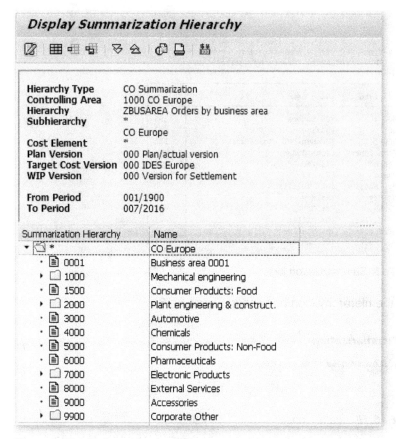

Figure 6.17: Initial report output

By opening the folder, the person responsible is displayed as seen in Figure 6.18.

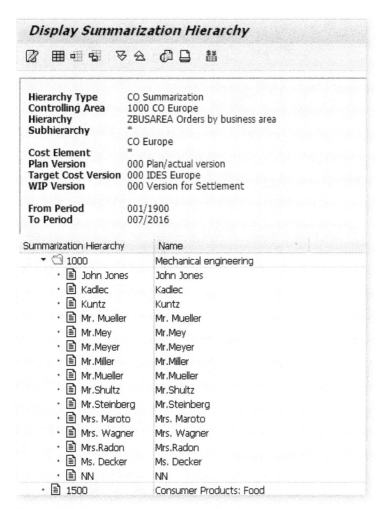

Figure 6.18: Expand folder to see next level

Adding a layout to the report will give it structure and display any available values, as seen in Figure 6.19.

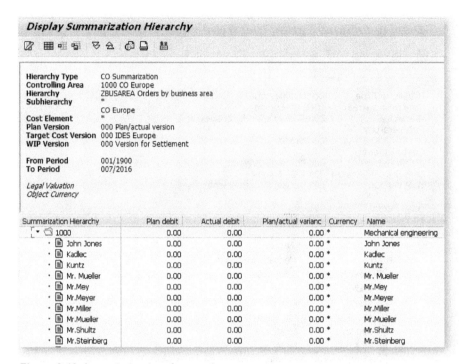

Figure 6.19: Layout structure in report

6.4   Summarization Customizing

To create a summarization hierarchy, from the IMG menu:

CONTROLLING • INTERNAL ORDERS • INFORMATION SYSTEM • SUMMARIZATION • MAINTAIN SUMMARIZATION HIERARCHIES KKR0

Select the NEW ENTRIES pushbutton.

Enter an eight-character alphanumeric ID and description as seen in Figure 6.20.

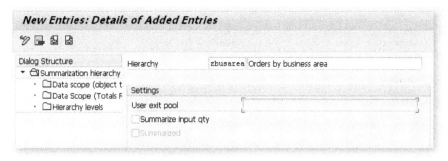

Figure 6.20: Create summarization hierarchy

In the DIALOG STRUCTURE to the left, select the DATA SCOPE (OBJECT TYPES) folder.

In this view, we indicate which types of orders we want to summarize.

As seen in Figure 6.21, select the checkbox for internal orders. Note that you can also indicate a status profile and a selection variant for the hierarchy.

Hierarchy	Description	Summar...	Prio.	Status...	Sel. variant	
ZBUSAREA	Internal Orders	☑	1			
ZBUSAREA	Maintenance/Service Orders	☐	2			
ZBUSAREA	Prod. Orders, QM Orders, Prod. Cost Coll	☐	3			
ZBUSAREA	Projects	☐	4			
ZBUSAREA	Sales Orders Without Dependent Orders	☐	5			
ZBUSAREA	Sales Orders with Dependent Orders	☐	6			

Figure 6.21: Selection of Internal Orders

In the DIALOG STRUCTURE to the left, select the HIERARCHY LEVELS folder.

In this view, we assign the master data fields to create the hierarchical structure. A controlling area will always be here by default.

Select the NEW ENTRIES pushbutton.

Using the dropdown in the hierarchy field, select the fields you want to use. As seen in Figure 6.22, in this example we are creating the hierarchy by business area and person responsible.

Hierarchy	Level	Hierarchy Field	Name	Tot...	Offset	Lngth	Blank
ZBUSAREA	2	GSBER	Business Area	4		4	☐
ZBUSAREA	3	USER2	Person Responsible	20		20	☐
ZBUSAREA	4			0			☐
ZBUSAREA	5			0			☐
ZBUSAREA	6			0			☐
ZBUSAREA	7			0			☐
ZBUSAREA	8			0			☐
ZBUSAREA	9			0			☐

Figure 6.22: Select the fields for hierarchy

Exception reporting

You can also utilize color thresholds in the reports by creating an exception in the next menu option: DEFINE EXCEPTION RULES.

Once the hierarchy is complete, execute transaction KKRC on the application menu to populate the summarization. Refer to Summarization Tools for the process steps.

7 Special Topics

In our final chapter, let's review a few optional features of internal orders and consider the impact of S4/HANA Finance.

7.1 Statistical Internal Orders

Statistical internal orders are used to provide another level of detail for analyzing cost. Since the order is not a real or true cost object, when posting to the order you must also enter a real or true cost object.

These orders have a variety of uses.

Expense by vehicle/fleet

 Assume you are the cost center manager for the Motor Pool. You want to track cost for each vehicle in the pool, while posting costs to the Motor Pool cost center. Creation of a statistical internal order for each vehicle supports this requirement. When costs are posted, each document must contain the Motor Pool cost center and the statistical vehicle order.

Expense by salesperson

 Assume you are the cost center manager for Sales. You want to track cost for each salesperson, while posting costs to the Sales cost center. Creation of a statistical internal order for each salesperson supports this requirement. When costs are posted, each document must contain the Sales cost center and the statistical salesperson order.

As seen in Figure 7.1, statistical orders must have the statistical indicator selected on the master record.

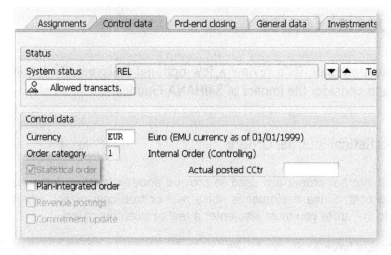

Figure 7.1: Statistical order indicator

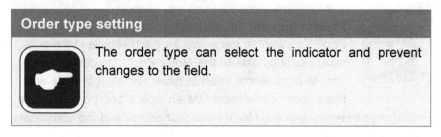

Settlement rules cannot be added to statistical internal orders. All real or true cost is posted to the real cost object on the entry. The statistical order information is for reference only.

Statistical orders can be analyzed in the information system using all of the reports in the menu.

7.2 Internal Orders with Revenue

It is possible to manage revenue on an internal order. First, the order type would need the revenue indicator selected. Then there are additional settings to consider:

▶ The settlement profile may require unique allocation and source structures as discussed in Settlement Customizing.

▶ Results analysis versions must be created in customizing.

▶ Additional settlement steps are required at Period End Close. They are found in the RESULTS ANALYSIS section of the application menu.

7.3   S4/HANA Simple Finance

As of this writing, SAP's most recent product offering is S4/HANA Simple Finance. There are many process improvements built into this product.

As relates to this manuscript, there are few changes to mention. In S4/HANA Simple Finance there is now a universal journal containing all FI and CO values. This data resides in a new table ACDOCA, and the tables COSS, COSP, as well as COEP, are removed.

From a user perspective, there are several new transaction codes for efficient HANA processing. Please consult the most recent updates in SAP Note 1946054.

There is also a Fiori user interface, with app-like features for transactions and reporting.

Reporting is improved by the elimination of aggregate tables and replacing them in "views." These new features may replace older ones, such as the summarization hierarchy.

You have finished the book.

A   The Author

Marjorie Wright is an accomplished subject matter expert, author, and speaker, and is the founder of Simply FI-CO, LLC, a boutique SAP training consulting company. She is an education consultant in the components of Financial Accounting, Management Accounting, and Financial Supply Chain Management. With more than 25 years of training and accounting experience across multiple industries including financial services, manufacturing, technology, utilities, telecommunications and healthcare, she has conducted training for more than 3,500 learners in traditional face-to-face classrooms, as well as in Web-based virtual meeting rooms.

B Index

C Disclaimer

This publication contains references to the products of SAP SE.

SAP, R/3, SAP NetWeaver, Duet, PartnerEdge, ByDesign, SAP BusinessObjects Explorer, StreamWork, and other SAP products and services mentioned herein as well as their respective logos are trademarks or registered trademarks of SAP SE in Germany and other countries.

Business Objects and the Business Objects logo, BusinessObjects, Crystal Reports, Crystal Decisions, Web Intelligence, Xcelsius, and other Business Objects products and services mentioned herein as well as their respective logos are trademarks or registered trademarks of Business Objects Software Ltd. Business Objects is an SAP company.

Sybase and Adaptive Server, iAnywhere, Sybase 365, SQL Anywhere, and other Sybase products and services mentioned herein as well as their respective logos are trademarks or registered trademarks of Sybase, Inc. Sybase is an SAP company.

SAP SE is neither the author nor the publisher of this publication and is not responsible for its content. SAP Group shall not be liable for errors or omissions with respect to the materials. The only warranties for SAP Group products and services are those that are set forth in the express warranty statements accompanying such products and services, if any. Nothing herein should be construed as constituting an additional warranty.

More Espresso Tutorials Books

Martin Munzel:

New SAP® Controlling Planning Interface

▶ Introduction to Netweaver Business Client
▶ Flexible Planning Layouts
▶ Plan Data Upload from Excel

http://5011.espresso-tutorials.com

Michael Esser:

Investment Project Controlling with SAP®

▶ SAP ERP functionality for investment controlling
▶ Concepts, roles and different scenarios
▶ Effective planning and reporting

http://5008.espresso-tutorials.com

Stefan Eifler:

Quick Guide to SAP® CO-PA (Profitability Analysis)

▶ Basic organizational entities and master data
▶ Define the actual value flow
▶ Set up a planning environment
▶ Create your own reports

http://5018.espresso-tutorials.com

Paul Ovigele:

Reconciling SAP® CO-PA to the General Ledger

- ▶ Learn the Difference between Costing-based and Accounting-based CO-PA
- ▶ Walk through Various Value Flows into CO-PA
- ▶ Match the Cost-of-Sales Account with Corresponding Value Fields in CO-PA

http://5040.espresso-tutorials.com

Tanya Duncan:

Practical Guide to SAP® CO-PC (Product Cost Controlling)

- ▶ Cost Center Planning Process and Costing Run Execution
- ▶ Actual Cost Analysis & Reporting
- ▶ Controlling Master Data
- ▶ Month End Processes in Details

http://5064.espresso-tutorials.com

Ashish Sampat:

First Steps in SAP® Controlling (CO)

- ▶ Cost center and product cost planning and actual cost flow
- ▶ Best practices for cost absorption using Product Cost Controlling
- ▶ Month-end closing activities in SAP Controlling
- ▶ Examples and screenshots based on a case study approach

http://5069.espresso-tutorials.com

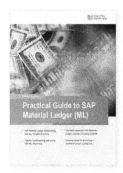

Rosana Fonseca:

Practical Guide to SAP® Material Ledger (ML)

▶ SAP Material Ledger functionality and key integration points

▶ Tips for implementing and using SAP ML effectively

▶ The most important SAP Material Ledger reports, including CKM3N

▶ Detailed steps for executing a multilevel actual costing run

http://5116.espresso-tutorials.com

Ashish Sampat:

Expert Tips to Unleash the Full Potential of SAP® Controlling

▶ Optimize SAP ERP Controlling configuration, reconciliation, and reporting

▶ Transaction processing tips to ensure accurate data capture

▶ Instructions for avoiding common month-end close pain points

▶ Reporting and reconciliation best practices

http://5140.espresso-tutorials.com

John Pringle:

Practical Guide to SAP® Profit Center Accounting

▶ Fundamentals of SAP Profit Center Accounting (PCA)

▶ Concepts, master data, actual data flow, and planning basics

▶ Differences between PCA in classic and new GL

▶ Reporting for Profit Center Accounting (PCA)

http://5144.espresso-tutorials.com/

www.ingramcontent.com/pod-product-compliance
Lightning Source LLC
Chambersburg PA
CBHW071204050326
40689CB00011B/2236